P9-BZT-120

"This is a much-needed book. The anxiety in making a life changing decision is sometimes overwhelming. It is of immense help to have a coach like Susan Pease Gadoua!"

—John Bradshaw, best-selling author of *Homecoming* and *Creating Love*

"Better than therapy! Pease Gadoua allows the reader who is contemplating any great change to process the pros and cons in the confines of his or her own heart and mind, leaving no chance for those on the fence to skip out on the truth. A must-read for any transition."

—Joan Anderson, best-selling author of *A Year by the Sea*, *An Unfinished Marriage*, *A Walk on the Beach*, and *The Second Journey*

"Making an appointment to see a divorce lawyer doesn't mean that the person I am advising necessarily needs or wants a divorce. With Pease Gadoua's wise, thorough, and accessible book, Contemplating Divorce, at last there is a resource I can give to confused and unhappy clients who think the marriage may be over but can't decide whether the embers are truly dead or not."

—Pauline H. Tesler, author of *Collaborative Divorce* and *Collaborative Law*

"An exceptional and outstanding book for all those considering making the life-altering decision to divorce. Pease Gadoua offers profound personal insight and practical guidance that empowers adults to find clarity, overcome hurdles, and make the best choices for the future of their relationships. I wholeheartedly recommend Contemplating Divorce to men and women alike."

—Helene Taylor, Esq., president and founder of TheModernWomansDivorceGuide.com

How refreshing to find a book that so carefully and thoughtfully addresses the myriad forces and pitfalls one faces when contemplating the life-changing decision to divorce. Susan Pease Gadoua gently guides the reader through the essential stages of decision-making to stay or go with dozens of helpful examples and self-tests. I highly recommend this book.

—Isolina Ricci, Ph.D., author of *Mom's House, Dad's House for Kids* and *Mom's House, Dad's House*

Contemplating

Di♥orce

A Step-by-Step
Guide to Deciding Whether
to Stay or Go

SUSAN PEASE GADOUA, LCSW

New Harbinger Publications, Inc.

Publisher's Note

This publication is designed to provide accurate and authoritative information in regard to the subject matter covered. It is sold with the understanding that the publisher is not engaged in rendering psychological, financial, legal, or other professional services. If expert assistance or counseling is needed, the services of a competent professional should be sought.

Distributed in Canada by Raincoast Books

Copyright © 2008 by Susan Pease Gadoua

New Harbinger Publications, Inc.
5674 Shattuck Avenue
Oakland, CA 94609
www.newharbinger.com

All Rights Reserved
Printed in the United States of America

Acquired by Melissa Kirk; Cover and text design by Amy Shoup; Edited by Nelda Street

---

Library of Congress Cataloging-in-Publication Data

Gadoua, Susan Pease.
    Contemplating divorce : a step-by-step guide to deciding whether to stay or go / Susan Pease Gadoua.
        p. cm.
    Includes bibliographical references.
    ISBN-13: 978-1-57224-524-2 (pbk. : alk. paper)
    ISBN-10: 1-57224-524-7 (pbk. : alk. paper) 1. Divorce.
2. Divorce--Psychological aspects. I. Title.
    HQ814.G33 2008
    306.89--dc22

                        2008016263

16 15 14
15 14 13 12 11 10 9 8

Contents

Acknowledgments

I'd like to thank my husband, Michael, for his amazing love, support, and feedback during the writing process.

I'd also like to thank Leslie Keenan, my friend, editor, and writing coach, for her knowledge, wisdom, and humor each week (and more when I needed it).

My thanks to those who have helped me all along the way by proofreading and sharing information with me: Susan Bross, Suzan Barrie Aiken, and Rodney Johnson. I'd like to thank my friends Kristin Morrison, Maureen Smith, Katherine Deiter, Lorraine Platt, Cynthia Stanley, and Shakti Gawain for their ongoing support and inspiration. Thanks to my sisters, Linda, Anne, and Nancy, and my brother, Ted, and, of course, my parents, Chuck and Louise.

I want to acknowledge the hard work of Melissa Kirk and Jess Beebe (and behind-the-scenes Nelda Street) from New Harbinger Publications, as well as Catharine Sutker, for opening the door of this opportunity to me. Thank you.

Finally, I would be remiss if I didn't thank and acknowledge the many women and men who have shared their personal stories with me and entrusted me during perhaps their most difficult life transition.

Introduction

Adversity does not build character. Adversity reveals character.

—Sandy Dahl (widow of Jason Dahl, captain of United Airlines Flight 93 on September 11, 2001)

*M*y involvement in divorce started at age nineteen in 1980, when my parents separated. Twenty-eight years of marriage came to a head in one final argument. The proverbial straw that broke the camel's back was reached, ironically enough, on their twenty-eighth wedding anniversary. They simply couldn't hold the family together any longer.

I believe that, because my parents felt that divorce was only for the weak, and therefore not an option, they remained married for many more years than they should have. Day after day and night after night, they fought, mercilessly tearing each other down. As children caught in this dynamic, my siblings and I suffered tremendously from our parents' unwillingness to accept that they were simply two very different people who no longer brought out the best in each other, if indeed they ever did.

While our parents meant well and I don't fault them for their choices, they didn't do us kids any favors by staying in the life of misery they generously deemed "matrimony." Many, if not most, nights I found myself wishing they would divorce, because, even as a young girl, I knew there had to be a better option than the constant fighting they engaged in. What they ended up modeling to us children was that marriage entails incredible sacrifice and a life sentence of suffering.

I was home for the summer when the actual breakup occurred but was entering my third year of college, so my primary residence was two and a half hours away. Because I was older, I did not experience the custody battles or schlepping of belongings from one house to another that younger children do. My life was relatively unaffected by my parents' divorce. It was only on the occasional visit back to my hometown when I felt the impact, and the relief, of my parents' decision to stop keeping up appearances and go their separate ways.

My mother and father were able to divide monetary assets and material possessions well enough, but there was a great deal of emotional wounding between them that I believe remains unhealed to this day. I say this partly because my mother spoke negatively about my father for *years* (more than twenty) after they divorced. She was masterful at turning a conversation around—even one about something totally unrelated to my father—to focus on how much he had wronged her and what a louse he had been all those years. Also she has never dated since then, nor has she seemed to have much interest in getting into another relationship. She appears to be beyond done with the love-and-marriage package.

On the other hand, my father sought comfort from the woman who is now his wife. While I don't believe that they had any physical affair prior to my parents' split, I think they had fallen in love and were having an emotional affair. My father moved right into his next marriage, never spending a day out of relationship.

By the time my parents got situated in their new lives, my college boyfriend and I were on the marriage track (as was expected of us). When I graduated, I moved in with Matt, who, being a year ahead of me, was already living on his own. We started talking about engagement and marriage. We picked out a diamond, and I received the family dress and the book *Emily Post's Wedding Etiquette* from my mother.

The stage was set, yet given my parents' example, I felt I would simply repeat history by marrying at age twenty-two. I would have my 2.5 children, be a stay-at-home mom, and feel miserable while Matt was off furthering his career. I had to get off that track. I told Matt I didn't want to get married yet, but he had his mind set on it. For him it was either now or never, and I had to choose. Although I truly did love him at the time, I just couldn't bear being "trapped" for the rest of my life. I chose to leave.

I spent the next twenty years as a single woman feeling judged and inadequate for never marrying. I felt judged because people would comment, "When are you going to get married so we don't have to worry about you anymore?" and "You've never been married? What's wrong with you?" Although it was my choice to avoid marrying just for the sake of marrying, the societal pressure was powerful.

As a married woman, I am treated quite differently. It seems ironic that I am more respected and viewed as a more complete adult now. Without question, we are a culture that values and encourages getting and staying married.

Divorce Is a Big Deal

In 2000 my intense interest in the subject of divorce was triggered again when I began working with divorcing women. What I quickly noticed was that divorce is often a messy process for those who must endure it. More times than not, the dissolution of marriage, even just the emotional disintegration of nuptials, brought out the worst in one or both spouses. The downward dynamic often involved partners falling out of love, yet feeling that there was no other option than to stay and suffer. It sometimes involved one partner lying, stealing, behaving unreasonably, and/or trying to bully the other into getting his or her way. In other instances, I observed partners creating drama and negativity so that they could feel justified in leaving the marriage. On rare occasions, clients told me that their split was mutual and amicable because they both realized they had simply grown apart.

In all my work as a therapist, I have never seen a population as lost, thrown off center, and frightened as this lot who were divorcing and contemplating divorce. Under normal circumstances, these people were strong, self-assured, responsible, and powerful, but when undertaking the marital dissolution process, these once confident and capable individuals fell to pieces.

Even other important life decisions or events my clients experienced—such as job transitions, major moves, loss of loved ones, and natural disasters—seemed less debilitating than divorce. It affected their sense of safety, well-being, community status, and comfort. Divorce *is* a big deal.

Every area of your life is affected by the breakdown of your marriage and family unit.

Rethinking Marriage and Divorce

While certainly not a divorce advocate, I don't believe divorce equals failure any more than I believe that staying married for fifty years necessarily means success. I also don't believe that it is wrong to leave a situation, regardless of what it is—a job, a neighborhood, a marriage—if it is killing your spirit.

We never know what goes on behind the closed doors of others. I often hear that a spouse showed his or her best face at parties and around others, only to dish out or endure incredible abuse when no one else was looking.

I am more impressed by the *quality* of the relationship behind those closed doors while it lasted than by its duration. Certainly, a long marriage is a testament to overcoming obstacles and the ability to "stick to it," but I would want to know at what expense a couple stayed together and why.

In this book, I will help you honestly assess the level of happiness and fulfillment in your marriage, and assist you in determining what more, if anything, you can do to improve your current situation. I'll call on you to choose to stay or go from a place of faith and following your truth, as opposed to staying or leaving out of fear. Every person on the planet has a different definition for "happy marriage." One person's ideal relationship might, to another, be the epitome of settling for less. Only you can make an honest appraisal of whether or not you're in the right marriage.

What This Book Offers You

I have written this book for the hundreds of thousands of people considering divorce and seeking clarity on what to do next, with or without their spouses. By providing a step-by-step guide of considerations, along with some personal stories and provocative exercises, I hope that all readers will come away with greater insights and acceptance about themselves and their relationships with their spouses.

This book is best read in the order written, simply because each step is listed in the order in which it's likely to appear in your process. The same holds true for the exercises. For example, you're not likely to have emotional ups and downs (chapter 3) until you have begun to seriously consider the idea of divorcing (chapter 1).

However, each chapter covers a separate topic, so each may be read separately. For topics you need to know more about, read those sections first. If you feel overwhelmed by thoughts or emotions at any point during your reading, I recommend that you put down the book for a while and come back to it when you feel stronger mentally and emotionally. There is no doubt that many intense thoughts and feelings will be stirred up for you throughout your reading. If you know to expect this, you will likely be more open to the guidance this book offers.

As with any self-help book, if you read each chapter two or three times, you will probably gain a new understanding each time you go over it, catching ideas that you missed the first time around. Your answers to the questions and exercises may change over time, as you get clearer with what you need and what direction you are headed in. I encourage you to repeat the exercises over time. I always recommend keeping a journal just for writing about your feelings as you go through this contemplation period. You can also use your journal to write out the exercises.

Prior to picking up *Contemplating Divorce: A Step-by-Step Guide to Deciding Whether to Stay or Go*, you may have felt as if you were about to burst at the seams and that you just wanted someone to tell you what to do. Unfortunately, it doesn't work that way. There are no quick fixes when deciding the fate of your marriage. All of the stories, exercises, and challenges included in this book are all that anyone can do to guide you and help you determine for yourself what to do. I hope that, along with imparting valuable information to you, this book will bring you a sense of comfort and support as you make this important decision.

Who Should Read This Book

Obviously, men and women who are contemplating divorce will want to read this book; however, I believe that anyone, even couples who are not in turmoil, can benefit from reading the chapter on relationship dynamics (see chapter 4). While *Contemplating Divorce* was written for husbands and wives, I believe it will help therapists, lawyers, clergy, doctors, and other professionals understand their clients better.

Steps in the Decision-Making Process

Like many processes, the divorce contemplation process entails a series of steps. Understanding these steps will make it easier to decide whether or not to stay in your marriage. They won't necessarily ease the emotional pain, but the steps are designed to bring a sense of order and normalcy to your contemplation process.

Each of the following steps will be explained in depth in its corresponding chapter:

1. Beginning the Mental Journey

2. Knowing Your Options

3. Understanding Your Emotions

4. Learning About Your Relationship

5. Knowing What You Need

6. Finding Your Truth

7. Taking Action When It's Needed

8. Understanding the Needs of Others

9. Making Peace with Your Decision

1

Beginning the Mental Journey

Is not marriage an open question when it is alleged from the beginning of the world that such as are in the institution wish to get out and such as are out wish to get in?

—Ralph Waldo Emerson

*Y*ou are reading this book because you have come to a place where you feel unhappy in your marriage. You probably feel as if you, your spouse, or both have failed or that something in your life has failed. You may sense that a part of you has died. And it probably has.

When you unhappily remain in any of life's situations, be it a job, a neighborhood, or a relationship, I believe that a part of you does die: the part of you that seeks a sense of aliveness—your spirit. One woman said recently that she felt as if she and her spouse were living a *Stepford Wives* existence: no love, no connection, and no emotion; rather, just going through the motions of being a family.

Feeling stuck with no remedy in sight usually results in some form of soul sickness. Even though you always have choices, it may not feel that way, because the choices you have at this juncture may seem less than ideal.

Standing on the precipice of such a big decision can be daunting. Feelings of sadness, guilt, fear, and anger are normal now, especially if your spouse is unaware of the extent of your unhappiness or you feel unsupported. You are not alone. There are hundreds of thousands of people feeling stuck in matrimonial confusion. No matter how difficult the circumstances you face, there is a solution.

While I can't tell you what the right answer is for you, through this book, I intend to help you clarify the best next step for you in your situation. I'll help you better understand your relationship, examine your motives for wanting to stay or leave, and look at the potential impact of whatever decision you make. Let's begin.

Standing at the Crossroads

Even just thinking about divorce may feel scary or bring feelings of betrayal of your spouse, yourself, your family, and your friends. Witnessing the growing divorce trends over the past few decades doesn't make marital dissolution any less difficult when it's a personal event rather than one endured by friends or neighbors.

Regardless of whether you tied the knot knowing full well that you could divorce someday if things didn't work out or believing that divorce would never be an option, you are now viewing your marriage and your life from a different perspective—one in which you are open to being unmarried to your spouse.

It would be highly unusual for a person to wake up one day and out of the blue say, "I want a divorce." Normally there's a whole series of events and emotional phases that one or both parties in a marriage experience before even beginning to consider marital dissolution.

Whatever your reason for coming to this place (you fought like cats and dogs, you changed but she didn't, you've become tired of a certain behavior or trait he has, or you've simply outgrown one another) or however long you've been unhappy or unfulfilled, you are reading this book because you need some guidance in your decision-making process.

The primary goal of this book is to help you sort out your emotions and assist you through the maze of confusion and grief you will undoubtedly experience. By the end of the last chapter, I hope that, with the road map provided here, you will have a clearer sense of what direction to take regarding your marriage. I hope that you will know more about yourself and your situation and that you will be armed with much more information about *how* to take steps to divorce if you choose to go this route.

There is no right or wrong way to go through the challenging decision of what to do next, but there are commonalities I've seen among those in marital flux.

The Divorce Contemplation Continuum

I have noticed that there are three distinct stages of consideration in marital dissolutions: precontemplation, contemplation, and postcontemplation.

Precontemplation

Precontemplation is when the notion to separate has just begun to develop. Someone at this stage may not think of divorce as a serious option but may feel that something is not working or have a vague sense that the relationship is off track. Precontemplation of marital dissolution usually begins after a series of smaller disagreements, one serious argument, or a betrayal of some kind. With all three of these scenarios, you may feel as if a line has been crossed but that it's not so egregious to make divorce a serious notion.

One example is Warren and Mimi, a couple who had only been married for eight months. They came to see me right after Warren found out that Mimi had not disclosed her arrest for "driving under the influence" just one year prior to their tying the knot. He wasn't upset about the DUI per se but was extremely concerned that she had not trusted him enough to tell him about it. He wondered whether, had he not opened a certain official-looking letter, she would've told him the truth. It also made him wonder what else she might have been withholding.

In reality, there was no reason for him to suspect that she was withholding anything further about this story, but it certainly threw a wrench into the relationship. Warren's first thought was that he couldn't trust Mimi and would have to divorce her. He eventually changed this line of thinking, and they were able to start over and rebuild trust.

At this stage, the idea of dissolving the marriage doesn't usually hang around long, nor does the one contemplating it spend too much time or energy imagining life as a divorced person. It is little more than a seed that has been planted in his or her mind.

Contemplation

Contemplation comes when the individual or couple has a much more serious need to consider divorce but perhaps needs more information to make a definitive decision. In this phase, it's not uncommon for the scales to be tipped one day at 85 percent toward staying and the next at 60 percent toward leaving, or vice versa. It's normal, although not necessarily comfortable, to experience a great deal of mental and emotional confusion at this stage. Because of its tumultuous nature, this stage can be extremely emotionally, mentally, and physically draining.

Postcontemplation

The final stage is postcontemplation, with or without resolution. Here, those considering divorce have either decided to stay in the marriage and stop questioning what to do next, leave the marriage (both of which include a form of resolution), or continue grappling with whether or not to stay.

With this last option, the person takes no action to find resolution, so the turmoil continues endlessly (without resolution). This latter group is painfully aware that their indecision hurts them, and perhaps their spouses and children as well, yet they remain stuck and cannot seem to move forward.

Are You In or Out?

If you are like most of the people I see, you are somewhere between contemplation and postcontemplation. A few of you may be in the precontemplation phase, but I find that most people don't start doing real footwork (such as reading books like this one) to make the choice to stay married or divorce until they have crossed the line into the contemplation stage.

Given that you are seriously considering leaving your spouse, you probably feel a great deal of fear—of the unknown, of pain, of doing irreparable damage to your children, of loneliness, of judgment, and on and on. We will explore many of these fears in depth later in the book, in hopes of assuaging them, but for the purpose of building a foundation of knowledge underneath you, I want to start with some information about the choices you have available to you at these crossroads.

What differentiates an unhappily married person who is contemplating divorce from someone who is simply unhappy with certain aspects of the marriage is the pair of glasses through which the relationship is viewed. In a typical marriage, there will be rough times and periods of discontent. When conflict arises, each spouse will feel normal frustration, upset, or anger, but in a healthy marriage, each will look *within* the marriage for the solution. When one or both partners have arrived at the place of contemplating divorce, they see *leaving the marriage* as a solution. Perhaps the person wanting out feels that he or she has tried other remedies to no avail or that the marital problems are much more serious than previously thought. In any case, one set of lenses (precontemplation) causes the person to look within the marriage for improvement, the other (contemplation and postcontemplation) without.

A small percentage of the population will jump right to the idea of leaving at the slightest hint of trouble. They don't see divorce as bad or wrong, perhaps because it is an accepted practice in their world or they got married too young, for the wrong reasons, or to the wrong person. These folks often know at the altar that they are not following their hearts, and may even enter their nuptials with an exit plan. They admit that they have made a mistake in their marriages and view divorce as the logical solution. There is not a lot of negativity surrounding the decision to divorce, because there wasn't much commitment to the marriage in the first place.

The other extreme is represented by those for whom, despite the tremendous amount and duration of unhappiness they experience, marital dissolution will never be an option. Sometimes this results from outside influences such as religious restrictions, cultural beliefs, or familial norms, but sometimes it is internal pressure from a personal desire to honor the vows exchanged, still feeling love for the spouse, or a number of other reasons we will explore in chapter 6. These folks would rather die or continue to suffer than divorce.

In these examples, marriage is either black or white: you can leave at the drop of a hat, or you are in it for life. Most people, even those who once thought they would be married forever but now face separation, live closer to the center of the continuum. Because there are more options in the middle, life is more complicated and it takes more effort to make decisions.

It can be agonizing to be in marital flux, not knowing what to do next. In fact, the most frustrating aspect during this process *is* the utter ambivalence and confusion that are present—often for quite a while. The indecision can be energy draining and crazy making for the person deciding, as well as those in close proximity.

It can feel like a form of insanity to be so convinced one minute that staying together and making things work is the best option, and the next minute want out; or to experience an amazing connection with your spouse one day and the following week want to throttle him or her, wondering what you ever saw in your spouse in the first place. Your friends and family may feel as if they are watching a Ping-Pong match, and yes, they may think you are at least temporarily insane. But this back-and-forth is quite common.

The Marital Indecision Cycle

Every marriage—and every meaningful relationship, for that matter—has good times and not-so-good times. This is natural and normal. However, when you are questioning whether to remain in the relationship, these high and low cycles may be more profound.

Not knowing the future of your marriage can feel as if you're riding on a roller coaster that you can never get off; there are endless ups and downs and loop-dee-loops. Although there are periods of calm, they are few, far between, and short lived.

After meeting with hundreds of clients who were contemplating divorce, I began to notice many similarities and a very predictable path that these people were following. This *marital indecision cycle*, as I call it, can feel like imprisonment, even though all it would take to be free would be to step off the merry-go-round.

FIGURE 1: THE MARITAL INDECISION CYCLE

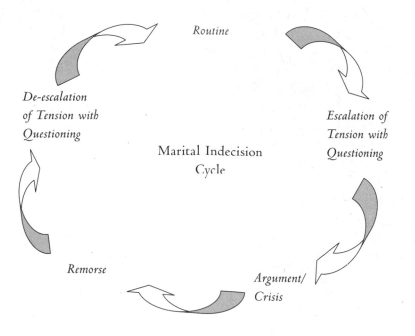

Routine

De-escalation
of Tension with
Questioning

Marital Indecision
Cycle

Escalation of
Tension with
Questioning

Remorse

Argument/
Crisis

Adapted from "The Cycle of Domestic Violence" in *The Battered Woman*, by Lenore Walker (1979, 55).

The marital indecision cycle begins with a calm or routine period followed by a slow buildup of tensions. There may or may not be questioning of the marriage at this juncture, but if there is, the questioning can actually add to the tensions and hasten the process of reaching the argument or crisis. After the argument or crisis, there is often remorse, followed by another questioning period, but this diminishes as tensions diminish over time, and eventually the routine phase returns. And the cycle repeats.

■ *Case Example:* Conrad's Story

Conrad came to see me because he was at wit's end with his unhappy marriage. He wanted to learn about the divorce process so he could move forward with it and start living again.

We talked for a while, and I gathered the background on his case. He seemed a bit anxious, so I asked him what was going on. He told me that this time he was really going to go through with it. I asked him what he meant by that, and he responded that he had been at this juncture a number of times before and that every time he felt absolutely ready to jump and convinced that he should, some outside influence came in and changed his course. Examples he gave included his wife's falling ill, their daughter's moving back in with them temporarily, and, ironically, their twenty-fifth wedding anniversary.

His anxiety resulted from his fear that, if he didn't hurry up and take this leap, something else would happen or he would change his mind again. He told me that every time he "returned" to the marriage, he hated himself. He added that his indecision was beginning to wear away at his self-esteem, and the longer he procrastinated acting on what he believed was inevitable, the more he lost respect for himself.

I showed Conrad the marital indecision cycle (see figure 1) and explained to him that the back-and-forth was a normal part of the process. Although that made him feel better, he still expressed a desire to get off the roller coaster. It was clear in Conrad's mind that he wanted out of his marriage. Much of the work he did with me was in uncovering whatever negative self-talk was getting in the way of his happiness. The loop he was caught up in was of his own making.

Conrad could finally see how he had set himself up to be unhappy by not setting clear limits with others and taking a stand for himself. On top of this important realization, he also saw that he behaved this way in his work life, with friends, and in virtually every relationship he had. These revelations were liberating for Conrad, and I watched him become strong enough to tell his wife that, indeed, he did want to divorce. It was not an easy transition for them to make, but his wife knew on some level that he had not been totally present. She supported Conrad to be true to himself and consented to divorce him.

What we witness in Conrad's story is his feeling trapped in the cycle and being unable to break out easily. He articulated well the impact of this endless round-and-round on him. It can be as frustrating to watch someone you care about struggle to end a relationship as to be in the loop yourself.

In this next case example of Lydia and Steve, we can see the events that led to Lydia's decision to leave her husband. We have a better sense of how worn down a person can become by not only the desire to leave but also the unhealthy dynamics causing the marriage's deterioration in the first place.

■ *Case Example:* Lydia and Steve's Story

Lydia joined one of my women's divorce groups a year and a half before she even started seriously considering filing for divorce from Steve. She was beyond the precontemplation phase but frozen by her ambivalence. She hoped that by joining a group she could gain insight on what to do next.

Lydia and Steve had been married for nine years and had two sons. This was his first marriage and her second. Given that she had been through divorce before, she wasn't looking forward to potentially going through the process again, and was primarily concerned that her family would ostracize her and regard her as bringing them shame and dishonor. She was also worried about what her friends and the other parents at her kids' schools thought, but much less than her family, whose conservative cultural and religious beliefs discouraged divorce.

When Lydia first came in, she shared that she was thinking about divorcing Steve because he was pulling some stunts that she didn't particularly like, such as staying out late, spending quite a lot of time with the mother of their son's best friend, and taking joint funds and funneling them into a property he had bought against her wishes.

She felt that he was pushing her away, which made her angry. Yet her anger made him distance himself even further. Although tension levels were always high in the house, Lydia was grateful that Steve had not reverted to his past drug use. She let the group know that that was her bottom line. She had been through an immensely difficult time with Steve when he was using drugs five years earlier, and she was not up for that again.

One evening, Lydia came in and announced to the group that she had evidence that not only was Steve using drugs again, but also he had driven under the influence with their two kids in the car. She was irate, yet not once did she mention the "D" word.

When one of the group members gently reminded her that she had previously set Steve's using drugs again as her bottom line, Lydia broke down in tears. She acknowledged having said that, but even as mad as she was now, she still didn't know if she could go through with it. She said she wished Steve would make the first move so that she wouldn't have to, since it was obvious that he wanted out of the marriage as well. That way, she wouldn't have to be the "bad guy" in her family's eyes.

But Lydia's saga continued. Week after week she came to group and vented about the latest happenings. She received unconditional support from the group, and slowly but surely, worked up the strength to file her divorce papers in court. By the time she reached the tipping point, it was months later and she had been through the wringer. She was beyond tired.

Looking back, Lydia saw that she had been beating a dead horse and that by trying to force their marriage to work, she and Steve had actually added layers of damage both to themselves and the children. The only benefit that seemed to come as a result of prolonging the agony was that Lydia was 100 percent sure that they had done all they could to keep the marriage together.

Debbie Ford articulates Lydia and Steve's process well. She writes: "Discontent occurs when our outer experiences aren't matching our inner desires.... In its early stages, discontent is fairly easy to overlook or conceal from ourselves. But like a glowing ember, the heat of discontent builds slowly over time until it becomes a blazing fire that can no longer be ignored. By then our discontent captures our full attention, and hopefully, we are motivated into action" (Ford 2005).

Perhaps you are at the earlier stages of your decision-making process or ready to take action to leave or resolve yourself to stay, but in either case the way will be made clearer for you as you read on.

Exercise: Where Are You and How Did You Get Here?

As with any journey, you need to know where you are starting from to know which direction to head in or how far you have to go to reach your goal.

The following questions are meant to give you a reference point as you proceed in making your decision. Answer each question in your journal. Because of the importance of knowing your starting point, complete this exercise as soon as you can. If you are unsure how to respond to something, skip the question for now and come back to it later. It may be that your marital picture will become clearer to you as you read further in this book. (Note: To get the maximum benefit from this exercise, answer questions 4 and 6 once a week for three months, and see if you notice a pattern of ups and downs or whether you have consistent feelings about your marital situation.)

1. How long have you been married?

2. Why are you considering divorce?

3. How long have you been considering leaving your spouse?

4. Where are you on the divorce contemplation continuum? (Circle one. If necessary, review the section "The Divorce Contemplation Continuum" earlier in this chapter before completing this step.)

1	2	3	4	5	6	7	8	9	10
Precontemplation				Contemplation			Postcontemplation		

5. Have you experienced the marital indecision cycle? Describe what that has been like for you.

6. As of this moment, where are you in the marital indecision cycle? (Circle all that apply.)

Routine   *Escalation of Tension with Questioning*

Argument/Crisis   *Remorse*

De-escalation of Tension with Questioning

7. In column A, make a list of concerns or complaints you have or have had about your spouse or about your marriage. In column B, write what you, your spouse, or both of you have tried to do to resolve the concern or complaint. Finally, in column C, state the outcome of each intervention.

A Concern/ Complaint	B Intervention	C Outcome
_____	_____	_____
_____	_____	_____
_____	_____	_____
_____	_____	_____

8. When you see the history of interventions that you and your spouse have employed, do you feel hopeful that things can change, or do you feel discouraged? Describe your feelings.

After completing this first series of questions, I hope you have a greater awareness of where you now stand with your marriage. There is much information in the following pages to help you learn about why you are where you are and how you got there. As you read on, keep an open mind. As you learn more about the dynamics of relationships, you may realize that you can change more than you thought you could. It will be important to come back to these questions once you have read the entire book to see if your answers and awareness have changed, and how.

2

Knowing Your Options

There are two primary choices in life: to accept conditions as they exist or accept the responsibility for changing them.

—Denis Waitley

Any decision you ever make in life, especially one as big as whether or not to divorce, will always be a better one if you make it a point to be informed about all your available choices. Everyone benefits when you have a better understanding of yourself, your marriage, and what it means to divorce. You can't know what the future holds, but studying your options and hearing others' stories can be greatly empowering so that you can absolutely have more say in how your situation turns out.

Options

While no option is ideal at this point in your marriage, all of your choices are fairly straightforward: you can stay married, you can separate, or you can divorce.

Staying in Your Marriage

We don't just arrive at a partnership that feels good and then rest. All marriages take work. By work, I mean that you have to give the relationship time and attention to build and maintain a solid base. What this foundation consists of will vary somewhat for each couple, but generally, deeper relationships are formed from the presence of qualities such as attraction (physical, mental, emotional, or spiritual), trust, honesty, compatibility, and respect.

Because every relationship is a living entity, you must continually do what you can to create a partnership that feels good to both of you, as well as to your children if you have any. Some of the basic components that make up a successful relationship include maintaining mutual honesty, respect, trust, and commitment. You may have your own personal version or twist on what is important (and we'll explore this in the exercise at the end of this chapter), but the point is that you and your spouse ideally do what you can to bring out the best in each other.

Relationships naturally have up and down cycles. Often, the bad stretches eventually pass. When you know this and expect that there will be some rough times in your marriage, you can more easily weather the discomfort you will experience during these periods. A couple who persists through the difficulties will usually tell you that their relationship is actually deeper and stronger than it was prior to this tough time and that it was worth hanging in there.

But what does a couple do when the trouble in their marriage is big trouble or when it lasts for a very long time? In my experience, those who are intent on staying married generally do one of three things: ignore the problem and hope it goes away, try to work on the issues themselves, or seek outside help.

IGNORING IT AND HOPING IT WILL GO AWAY

Although it may sound silly, you do have the option to do nothing and hope things improve. Sometimes, putting the problems on the back burner does make issues go away for a period, but in most cases they usually resurface somewhere down the road.

There is something to be said for picking your battles and not sweating the small stuff, but when there's a significant issue coming between you and your spouse, sticking your head in the sand will not resolve anything. It may just temporarily take the energy away from the problem, making it merely appear to be resolved.

Hope springs eternal, and the idea that staying in the marriage and waiting might just shift something is a powerful lure that many people fall prey to. It is often only when a great deal of time has passed and you see that nothing has changed that you realize you should have taken action sooner.

One of the dangers of ignoring problems or doing nothing to change things in your relationship when change is clearly needed is that one or both partners may unconsciously create a crisis. This is an event that crosses the line in a marriage and tests the nature of its existence. Examples of these crises include affairs, financial disasters, job losses, addiction, and mental or emotional breakdowns.

Not everyone who creates or contributes to these types of situations does so simply because he or she unconsciously wants the marriage to end, but the boundaries of acceptable and respectable behavior in the marriage are certainly stretched. So much damage can result from these interactions that divorce is unquestionably and understandably invited in.

For those of you who want to consciously and actively work on the issues rather than ignore them, you can do that in one of two ways: work things out together without outside help (which I call *inside intervention*) or employ resources outside your marriage to help you (*outside intervention*).

Staying in your marriage using inside intervention: Inside intervention can take many forms. It can be spouses learning about and implementing new ways of communicating, connecting, and resolving whatever obstacles have arisen in the relationship. Although self-help books technically are resources found outside of the couple, I include these as inside interventions because, presumably, it is still just the husband and wife trying to work things out together without consulting professional help. New ideas are introduced through the literature, but no outside person is involved.

Another example of inside intervention is creating something new in the relationship, such as a career change. New jobs, new homes, and new children are positive ways some couples can find a new focus and therefore often come together to resolve their issues. These changes can be the very thing the marriage needs to get back on track.

A case in point is a woman I once worked with named Marie, whose marriage had been rocky from the beginning. Although friends and relatives warned the couple not to have children, they decided to get pregnant. It was a definite adjustment early on, but this couple actually became closer by creating a "parenting partnership," as they called it.

The majority of husbands and wives who have kids as a way to save the marriage find that more strain is placed on the relationship, making matters worse. This couple was the exception to the rule, and they felt quite fortunate.

Another situation involves a couple I consulted with who described their relief when their cross-country move for his new job brought the changes they had hoped would save their marriage. The period immediately following the move was unsettling, which was what motivated them to seek counseling. Both spouses questioned what was keeping them together. However, because the move helped separate them from some toxic family influences, they realized that they had a genuinely loving and fulfilling marriage.

Staying in your marriage using outside intervention: Interventions such as marital therapy, spiritual or religious counseling, trial separation, or legal mediation are powerful tools couples can bring to their relationships to improve or save the marriage. However, people sometimes have unrealistic expectations of how much these outside influences can accomplish. What couples should keep in mind is that the success rate of any intervention they employ, regardless of what it is or how capable the professional whom they are working with is, will only be as good as *both* spouses' levels of motivation.

Many people have come to me for marriage therapy hoping that I could wield some power over their spouses that they themselves didn't possess, and get them to listen or change in some way. Certainly, objective input from a professional trained to deal with such matters can help, but it is important to understand that there is no magic cure.

If you are currently attempting to manipulate your spouse in hopes of getting a particular result, just know that this action is not likely to be effective and can sometimes do more harm than good.

■ *Case Example:* Terry and Eric's Story

Terry's husband, Eric, was a fierce workaholic, and she was having trouble dealing with their two sons (who were seriously acting out) by herself. She tried to get Eric into therapy and a Workaholics Anonymous group, and even hired an interventionist, who staged a full-blown intervention with friends and family.

Eric was so engrossed in his addiction that he only saw Terry and the rest of the interveners as a threat to his "success and passion." Rather than choosing to stop his destructive work habits, he left Terry and their two kids; stopped speaking to his parents, siblings, and best friend; and virtually disappeared. After all was said and done, Terry had less support from Eric than before she started attempting to control his workaholism.

Regardless of the behavior or trait that your spouse displays, for your influence to have any type of long-lasting impact, it must be because *your spouse* wants to make this change for him- or herself.

Many people ask me how they can get their spouses to stop using drugs or alcohol, get them out of their depression, prevent them from cheating again, or get them to be more emotionally available.

No doctor, therapist, clergy, or magician in the world can help you change anyone who doesn't want to change. Nor can any professional have a direct impact on that person if he or she doesn't see the value of changing. As we say in substance-abuse interventions, "When someone is not ready to stop a behavior, you can't say the right thing, and when someone is ready, you can't say the wrong thing."

My response to those who ask how they can best influence their partners is always the same: the most powerful impact you can have on another person is to work on yourself. This reply usually takes people aback, because it's not at all what they came to me to learn about. But it's the truth. The most influential way you can help shape others is to change *your* thoughts, behaviors, attitudes, and assumptions; be a good role model; and work harder on yourself.

Because it often only takes one person to change for a family or interrelational-group system to be altered, invariably everything and everyone has the potential to improve, even if just one piece of the equation improves. Others will soon start reacting differently to your new behaviors. They will respect you more, listen to you better, and enjoy interacting with you more. An added benefit of keeping the focus on yourself is that you are no longer viewed as the "bad guy" or nag in your partner's eyes. Instead, your spouse is often forced to start looking at him- or herself.

This doesn't mean that you necessarily have to ignore or condone unacceptable behavior from others, but when you keep the focus on yourself, the bulk of your time and energy is used to change yourself, not people or circumstances over which you have no control.

No change happens overnight, especially when a pattern has been in place for many years. It may take time for those around you to understand that you have changed and that you are serious about your new bottom line or request.

■ *Case Example:* Dan and Becky's Story

Several years ago, a man I know named Dan grew tired of the negative dynamic he and his wife, Becky, often engaged in whenever they had both had a few too many drinks. He decided that he wanted to get sober. Determined to change his life, he began attending Alcoholics Anonymous meetings and also got himself into therapy.

Becky, who on some level also knew that she habitually overindulged in alcohol, saw her husband start to feel better, as well as change and grow. Dan made no comment or gesture to her that she should follow in his footsteps, but Becky quickly realized that if she didn't change and do some inner work herself, her marriage was over. She started attending AA meetings with him, and before they knew it, they were in couples counseling, working on some important issues that had kept them both unhappy, which, ironically enough, was one of the reasons they had turned to the bottle in the first place.

When Dan started to work on himself, he had the choice to impose his new belief system on Becky. He could have told her that he had found sobriety and, if she wanted to stay married to him, she'd better get sober, but he didn't. He decided that his welfare was not contingent on her joining him and also realized that his recovery was just that—his recovery, not hers.

Becky became curious about Dan's abstinent lifestyle. She saw that he felt better physically, looked better, and seemed to be happier. She noticed that they fought less. She wanted what he had, and because he didn't push his path on her, she had the room to move forward.

Nine years later, they are still married and have come through quite a lot together as a sober couple. They would be the first to tell you that their relationship is not perfect, but both agree that, had Dan chosen to be pushy, talk down to Becky, or try to manipulate her in any way, she would have done all she could to defy him. She even admitted that she was waiting for him to start, so she could rebel or even leave. In many ways, leaving would have been easier for her than looking at herself has been, though nowhere near as rewarding.

This story had a good ending in that both parties changed, grew, and became very committed to doing their own inner work (and continue to do so), which resulted in their staying together and becoming genuinely happy together.

Regardless of the circumstances or reasons why you are contemplating divorce, you will still likely feel scared, ambivalent, and unsure that marital dissolution is the way to go. As I mentioned earlier, every relationship has a difficult period from time to time, and when it is just a period, it does pass. It would be just as unfair to you and your spouse to move too quickly to end the marriage as to wait too long.

Separation

The gray area between staying married and divorcing is separating. What does this mean and what does it look like? There are more variations on this theme than any other, but most people don't usually opt for separation as a long-term solution. When we hear that a husband and wife are separating, most of us think that they are on their way to the divorce court. Couples who have reached this point have usually tried various interventions and tactics to get the marriage back on track, but nothing has worked. The marriage is in a state of disrepair, so now there is nothing left to do but split up, separate, and then divorce.

However, rather than a means to an end, separation can be a helpful tool to stay together. This seems counterintuitive when a marriage is troubled and relations are fragile. Most of us believe that when we feel our spouse slipping away from us, we should merge together more, get as close as we can, and do more to "make the marriage work."

The thought of creating distance at such a time instills a great deal of fear of losing control of your spouse and your relationship. This option is especially challenging if the bond between the two of you has been weakened by a betrayed trust. But, employed carefully and skillfully (and usually with some type of professional support), this tool can be quite effective in bringing two people closer together.

In this section, we'll explore the three main reasons why couples separate: to enhance their marriage, to gain perspective on their marriage, and to take a first step in the divorce process.

SEPARATION TO ENHANCE THE MARRIAGE

Separation between spouses does not always have to be incorporated just when the relationship is heading south. It can be used as a tool to improve relations. We're living in a time when there are many more variations on marriage than the traditional ideas we learned about in fairy tales or from older TV shows like *Father Knows Best*. Contemporary trends include couples living in separate towns for part of the time or living in the same town but in different homes.

Tom, a college professor, leaves his wife Laurie every September to teach the fall semester at a college in another part of the country. When he finishes teaching, he returns home to Laurie. Both Tom and Laurie cherish this arrangement because they have enough alone time to feel autonomous and enough togetherness to feel married. They describe their marriage as very strong and state that it would probably not be as good if they lived together 365 days of the year. Living apart enhances their relationship.

Another couple, Jane and Sam, live in northern California. This couple seriously considered divorce because of different parenting styles. When Jane was offered a job in Los Angeles, she took it. Unsure whether marital dissolution was going to be the end result, Jane was reluctant to completely move out of their home in Napa, so instead she rented an apartment in Los Angeles. She stayed in Southern California Monday through Friday and commuted home to the wine country each weekend to be with Sam and the kids.

What they soon discovered was that, even though their parenting styles never quite meshed, there was less conflict, because Jane was away most of the time. Sam, who was a househusband, had charge of the kids during the week, and Jane wasn't there to contradict his parenting style.

There are other married couples who choose to live in separate residences, whether a town away or down the street from each other, to simultaneously maintain individuality and partnership.

Living apart doesn't absolve either party from having to work on the relationship. What is crucial to understand is that these arrangements succeed only when there is good mutual communication and honesty about what works and what doesn't. Each spouse trusts the other and shares the same expectations. They both enjoy a sense of autonomy while sharing the goal of creating a healthier connection with each other.

SEPARATION TO GAIN PERSPECTIVE ON THE MARRIAGE

In 1999, Joan Anderson wrote a book called *A Year by the Sea*, in which she tells the autobiographical story of living by herself at her summer house for a full year to determine whether or not she wanted to remain in her marriage. Ultimately, she decided to reconcile with her husband, and the clarity she gained by taking care of herself in this way had a positive and powerful impact on her and the rest of her family.

Sometimes couples actually gain this perspective through their willingness to let go of the relationship. Living apart allows them to step out of the muck and mire, and get onto higher ground.

■ *Case Example:* Linda and Jorge's Story

Linda and her husband of eighteen years, Jorge, had decided to separate, with the idea that they would eventually get divorced. Jorge moved to a small apartment nearby, and Linda stayed in the house.

From the moment they separated, they missed each other terribly. They continued to go on hikes and dates, and began to appreciate each other more. Despite the fact (perhaps because of it) that they were on a steady course toward dissolution, they came to realize the depth of their love and connection. Solidifying their friendship and working hard on themselves and on creating the relationship they truly wanted enabled them to turn the tide.

A year and a half after moving out, Jorge not only moved back in, but the couple renewed their vows. Now their marriage is stronger than ever.

This story illustrates a point I heard once: "You can't have a real relationship until you are willing to not have the relationship." What Linda and Jorge discovered in their time apart was that their love for each other was stronger than their need for each other. In their readiness to let go of the relationship, they could see their connection more clearly and objectively.

They saw that they could be quite self-sufficient and take care of themselves, thus reducing their unhealthy dependence on each other. They learned to take responsibility for themselves, did some much-needed inner work, and consequently stopped blaming each other for their problems. Their new bond was stronger, because both had become more honest, more mature, and more capable of giving and receiving love.

Couples can choose to implement such a nuptial time-out informally and on their own, or more formally and with professional guidance. In her book *Should I Stay or Go?* therapist Lee Raffel (1999, 10) helps couples create what she calls a "controlled separation." Following particular parameters (not unlike how an actual divorce situation would look, complete with temporary financial support, child custody visitations, and separate living quarters), each person agrees not to file for divorce during the controlled separation and to give the other as much distance as needed to get perspective or to heal past hurts. At the end of the agreed-upon term of separation (usually six months), the couple can reassess their goals with the hope of getting back together.

Of course, not everyone undergoing a controlled separation arrives at the decision to reunite, but it is a different spin on resolution that can be quite helpful to many couples.

Curt, the husband in a couple I worked with, told me that after his wife, Dianne, moved out, he felt such a sense of relief and renewed energy from being apart from her that he had no idea how he had lasted in the marriage for close to thirty years. For him, the break validated that leaving the relationship was the right decision.

The internal reactions people have to separating can be quite varied. However, this process will almost certainly bring you valuable information and insights about yourself and your relationship.

SEPARATION AS A STEP TOWARD DIVORCE

This is the form of separation that most people are familiar with. Couples who know they want to divorce have often lived with a great deal of discomfort or lack of fulfillment—and usually for a very long time—so being apart from their spouses can be welcome relief.

The split may be prompted by the fact that one or both partners have changed (or not changed), they are no longer in love, they no longer share common interests, a trust has been betrayed, or a crisis has caused them to reexamine their relationship.

These individuals or couples have crossed an invisible line of no return. While they may struggle with the "shoulds," such as "We should stay together because of the kids," they know in their hearts that the relationship is over.

When asked if there is any chance of reconciliation, they will give it anywhere from a 10 to 30 percent chance. It is a rare occasion when someone says that there is zero possibility of turning things around.

I surmise this, because with every major decision in life, there is a list of pros and cons that comes with the territory. Getting divorced is not necessarily a clear-cut or easy decision, even when there is tremendous abuse or neglect. Most people understand that they are trading in their uncomfortable "knowns" for some "unknowns," with no guarantee of any more happiness than the situation they are letting go of, but it is a chance they are willing to take to be more in alignment with their truths.

Once a couple is on the divorce track, the separation is not implemented with the purpose of getting a better perspective on the relationship (although this can happen, as you saw in Linda and Jorge's story); rather, it is part of the natural course as each party prepares to go his or her individual way. This is the "in-between" stage of the process.

Sometimes, living apart is necessary. The husband and wife can no longer reside under the same roof due to the level of anger, distrust, or animosity between them. Sometimes it just makes sense to begin the separation process by having one person move out. It can soften the contrast between being married and being divorced.

While not all couples live in separate dwellings during divorce proceedings, most do. In areas of the country where the cost of living is relatively high, some spouses have to live in the same house for economic reasons. This is often a temporary situation, and it's a rare couple who can actually continue living together after their divorce is finalized.

One housing option many parents choose these days to minimize the upheaval for their children is commonly referred to as "nesting." This is when each parent rotates moving in and out of the family home, while the children stay put. Each spouse may have his or her own apartment, separate from the other's apartment, or they may share the same apartment (since they aren't living there at the same time).

■ *Case Example:* Kerry and Mark's Story

Just how much physical distance each couple needs will vary. Kerry and Mark felt strongly that they needed to live apart but wanted to provide their children with as much continuity as possible. Mark moved out of the family house and into a house on the same block. This worked well in the short run, but things got a bit strange for them well after their divorce was finalized—when Mark started a new relationship.

Whenever Kerry passed by Mark's house and saw his new girlfriend's car in the driveway, she felt her stomach churn, even though she knew she didn't want to be in a relationship with him. What got to her was the idea that he had moved on and that she was replaceable. Within six months, Kerry decided that she would move to a different location within the same school district so that her children could continue their education without interruption and Mark's new relationship would not feel so "in her face."

In hindsight, Kerry wished that she had asked Mark to relocate farther away when they first split up, but at the time she wasn't thinking about the next chapter of their lives. It was hard enough to think about anything beyond the millions of immediate details this transition was creating.

■ *Case Example:* Bob and Katherine's Story

The other end of the spectrum of splitting up a family system can be likened to amputation, which can be equally unproductive. When Bob expressed to Katherine the dissatisfaction he felt with their marriage, he already had a new place to move into—thirty miles away from her.

For him, it was not if but, rather, when their divorce would happen, and he was simply taking care of business by cutting his ties with her as quickly as possible. Although Katherine agreed that their marriage left a great deal to be desired, she felt abandoned in his moving out and their abrupt separation.

She asked him to stay in the family home and even agreed to give him the master bedroom; she would sleep downstairs in the family room to integrate the changes in their relationship. Initially Bob complied, though against his better judgment. For him, quick, permanent good-byes were the easiest way to go.

They ended up living together that way throughout the entire divorce process (a little over nine months) and were able to delve into what went wrong in their marriage, discuss how they could maintain a friendship, and, more importantly, create a co-parenting plan, which never would have happened had Bob followed through on his impulse to immediately move so far away. He might have felt better in the moment but would have created very difficult circumstances in which to navigate and negotiate their divorce.

When you are considering ending your marriage, it is important to imagine what life might be like once the divorce actually happens and both spouses move on. Be as honest as you can with yourself and your partner, and try to maintain good relations. However, be aware that trying, at any cost, to preserve the sense of family to avoid hurting someone or maintain constancy for the kids can come back to haunt everyone later on.

Divorce

The decision to divorce is not an easy one, but no choice at this stage will be easy or without its own set of problems and issues. In this country, approximately half of all marriages end in dissolution, so it's clearly a path that many people choose.

Three factors distinguish this option from the others: the finality of this choice, its far-reaching life changes, and the stigma that may happen during and after divorce.

DIVORCE IS FINAL

Divorce marks the end of the family unit as you now know it. It is definite and complete. There are not usually second chances once this path is chosen. Even though we all hear stories of couples divorcing and then remarrying each other (for example, Elizabeth Taylor and Richard Burton), the reality is that the chances of spouses reuniting are slim to none. Most people move from their bad or unfulfilling marriages into new relationships or no relationship.

When couples have no children, the finality is even more pronounced. These individuals have little or no reason to stay in touch, unless they opt to remain friends. For some, this is welcome news. Being free of attachment to an ex-spouse one no longer loves and lives with is a big relief. Others feel a tremendous sense of loss because this person, who was once family, now holds the status of stranger. There is no contact, no knowledge of what the ex-spouse is up to, and there's no reason to maintain a connection. This stark and uncomfortable contrast can be troubling for quite a while.

If the couple has children, though their marital relationship changes drastically, they are bound forever as the parents of their children. Whether they communicate or get along is irrelevant. The children will always be their connection, and the ex-spouses will always be, in essence, family.

For many people, this type of tie is a major challenge. As my mother put it after splitting up with my father, "It's worse than a death, because the other person doesn't go away." The grieving can feel prolonged, because there is no "getting over" the loss of the spouse, the relationship, or the dashed dreams. He or she is always there, and you are required to interact with each other. This is true even if your children are grown. Like it or not, at various family events—graduations, weddings, births, and funerals—you will probably have to interact with your ex-spouse.

Some divorced couples find that they get along better after realizing and accepting that they shouldn't be married. Maybe co-parenting is a snap because they were always a good team in this regard. Or, the relationship is simply easier because both ex-partners are happier as two single individuals than as a married couple.

A former client named Christy recently contacted me to tell me that she had remarried. She went on to inform me that her ex-husband, Craig, had performed the wedding ceremony, since he was ordained as an interfaith minister. The guests were quite surprised by how well they all got along.

To boot, she said that her new husband, Brian, introduced Craig to a female friend of his named Debra, and now *they* planned to move in together. And the one who benefited most from all of these relationship changes was their thirteen-year-old daughter, whom Christy described as the "sanest, most well-adjusted girl I know."

DIVORCE IS FAR REACHING

If the mere thought of getting divorced overwhelms you, it is with good reason. I liken the divorce process to untangling the root system of two trees that have grown side by side. The more years of root growth they have experienced together, the more tangled and entwined their dissolution process will be. It is not easy, no matter what the circumstances, but this "old growth" can make it that much tougher.

Divorce will impact every single area of your life. And your new status as a single person usually makes every aspect of life more challenging, at least initially. It's not like quitting a job, wherein your time and money situations change but you still have the same place to come home to every day, with the same family. The impact of leaving your marriage permeates your family, home, finances, time management, and, in most cases, work life.

Divorce affects many others besides the two who are splitting up. Every member of the immediate family feels the repercussions of the changes that come with marital dissolution, as do the extended family; friends; neighbors; and sometimes even employers, employees, and coworkers.

The children of a divorcing couple are often shuttled back and forth between Mom's house and Dad's house. Pets may even be traded back and forth or be otherwise impacted by the changes.

Having two households can be quite costly, causing everyone to make sacrifices to afford the higher overhead. The children may have to go without soccer camp or tae kwon do, and the parents might have to eat out less often. Frequently, the family has no choice but to sell the house and downsize their entire lifestyle.

If one parent was not working during the marriage, he or she may be forced to start working to contribute income or go back to school to gain skills to earn a living. Some will have to get second jobs or be forced to change jobs for a higher-paying position.

Coworkers may have to pick up the slack for the divorcing person who must take time off for legal appointments or who is preoccupied with the intense emotions that accompany such loss. In more extreme cases, the divorcing person literally cannot function on the job and calls in sick more frequently.

Cathy was devastated when she got a less-than-glowing evaluation at her corporate job in the year of her divorce. She thought she had done well at keeping up appearances and putting whatever leftover energy she had into her work. Looking back, she realized that, because her divorce was so devastating to her, she couldn't possibly have been fully present and focused.

These are just some examples of the myriad of ways in which divorce affects people and their various situations. At this stage of your process, you may be able to foresee potential issues in some of these areas, but there will likely also be some ripples that wind up taking you by surprise.

It's certainly appropriate to have a healthy fear of such changes and to weigh all of the pros and cons to the extent possible before making the decision to divorce.

STIGMA

Even in our modern American culture, divorce is still seen as a negative life event—even taboo. Despite its fairly common occurrence, divorce isn't supposed to happen. It is considered a failure. Divorce tends to bring out the worst in people—everyone, not just the divorcing couple. The people around the couple, be they friends, family, or more distant acquaintances, may believe that the "disease" of divorce is contagious. Given that they don't want to "catch it," they may keep their distance from the divorcing individuals and withhold much-needed support.

Many people believe that anyone who has divorced once has issues, so anyone who has divorced more than once must have serious issues. I've heard someone described as "a three-time loser" because he had three "failed" marriages. Such reactions from others would elicit and add to the already-existing shame and bad feelings any divorcing person might have.

If divorce equals failure, then it stands to reason that, in society's eyes, marriage equals success—unless, of course, you are marrying for the second, third, or fourth time. But who sets these standards? Our way of thinking about love, romance, marriage, and divorce is influenced heavily by traditions, social norms, and mores that have become the foundation for many of the marital laws in place today.

What most people don't consider is that marriage has existed for thousands of years in many different forms and has evolved into what we know today from a variety of influences. Ironically, the view we currently hold on marriage and divorce is a relatively recent historical phenomenon, not just in our Western culture but throughout the world.

In today's world, we are expected to do more, be more, and have more. When it comes to marriage, this is no exception. In her book *Marriage, a History: How Love Conquered Marriage*, Stephanie Coontz (2005) comments that never before has any culture set such high standards for what marriage should be and do for a person and a society. In the last two hundred years, marriage has evolved from a union designed to meet only our most basic needs to an institution wherein all of our needs are expected to be taken care of. Husbands and wives in the Western world have come to expect their mates to satisfy and fulfill their every need—physical, social, emotional, and intellectual. Coontz believes that, although the intention of having marriage satisfy more of our needs was meant to strengthen the institution, the unrealistic nature of these expectations actually threatens the stability of marriage.

In other words, as marriage has evolved, our culture has inadvertently created a goal (uniting with a person who will meet all of your needs "till death do you part") that is difficult, if not impossible, to attain. Yet we unfairly stigmatize those who don't reach it.

I make this point here, not because I want to create a debate about whether the way we view marriage today is right or wrong but to help you see that your expectation of yourself and others to marry "forever after" is not very realistic.

I hope that knowing this information will change your perspective on your situation and help take away some or all of the judgment you may have toward yourself. I also hope you will feel less judged by others, even members of your own family.

It isn't easy to change your belief that divorce is bad or wrong when that message has been ingrained in our culture for so long, but it is important to take the element of judgment away so you can make a better decision about whether or not to stay in your marriage. This next story illustrates perfectly how easy it is to allow fear of judgment to dictate our actions.

■ *Case Example:* Rob and Jenny's Story

Rob and Jenny, who met through friends, admitted that they had married for less-than-great reasons. For her, it was that all of her friends were getting married (she was twenty-eight at the time), and for him, it was that getting married was simply what you did when you reached a certain age (he was thirty-two). It was the first marriage for both.

At one point Jenny confessed to me that she knew she shouldn't have married Rob but was caught up in all the festivities and celebratory mood of everyone from the minute the couple had announced their engagement all the way up to their wedding day. Both families had been ecstatic.

In hindsight, Rob and Jenny realized that having only dated for eight months prior to getting married was not a long enough time to see each other's true colors. Had they waited, they might have seen that, despite the love they felt for each other, they had virtually nothing in common. She liked to go out to clubs; he liked to stay home and watch TV. She loved to spend time and money shopping; he thought malls were a huge waste of space and abhorred spending his hard-earned money on the "little things." He was totally into his work and career, but to her, work was nothing more than a means to an end. Rob considered Jenny extremely immature, and Jenny thought Rob was a stick-in-the-mud.

Rob had sincerely wanted to marry Jenny and just assumed that being married and eventually having children would force Jenny to grow up and settle down. Jenny had also thought marriage would tame her, though she had no idea she would feel imprisoned.

Even the birth of their son, Zach, did not change Jenny. In fact, in some ways, she rebelled, because now two people threatened to take away her freedom. She was a great mother to her son when she was with him, but she was quite the party girl when someone else was taking care of him.

The demise of their marriage came one night when Jenny was out on the town with some girlfriends from work and met Gerard, a tall, dark, and handsome man for whom she fell head over heels. The affair began somewhat discreetly, but within a short time, people began to suspect something. Jenny was home less and less, and the burden of caring for Zach fell almost 100 percent on Rob's shoulders.

Both Rob and Jenny had expected that marriage would change her and calm her down, but it didn't. Rob had hoped that having a child would hold Jenny more accountable, but it didn't. Jenny had expected that her feelings for Rob would change and she would "grow into" being married, but she didn't. Both grew more resentful of each other and their situation. Both wanted things to change: he wanted her home more, and she wanted him off her back.

In less than two years, they had created a miserable existence, but both felt that they would really disappoint their respective families and friends, so they maintained the facade of being a happy couple for another eight months. Jenny was willing to betray her husband by having an extramarital affair, yet she was terrified of causing harm to their families by divorcing Rob.

Finally, they each had to admit defeat. The pain they experienced from hurting each other and living a lie was now greater than the shame and guilt they had feared. Jenny filed for divorce, and within six months the marriage was legally dissolved.

In Rob and Jenny's story, the couple married and stayed unhappily married for almost three years because they believed it was what they "had to do" as adults. Despite an inner knowing that they should split up, this young couple felt pressure from both sets of in-laws, friends, and even bosses to conform to the social marital norms.

Fear of being criticized by others is a powerful motivator, causing many people to try to avoid finding themselves in a position of being judged. However, when you allow the thoughts, feelings, and needs of others to outweigh your own, you are not being true to yourself.

Exercise: Contemplating Your Options

This exercise is designed to help you assess your ideal situation compared to your current reality, as well as help you examine the reasoning behind your desire to stay or go.

1. What is the *ideal* outcome to your current situation?

    Stay Married   Separate   Divorce   Other (Write it here.)

2. Why is this your ideal outcome?

3. Using the scale below, rate your *current* inclination with your marriage:

1	2	3	4	5	6	7	8	9	10
Divorce				Separation				Staying Married	

4. Why are you currently staying in your marriage?

As you may see from this exercise, your ideal outcome and your current reality don't necessarily match. Think about whether and how the real and the ideal can become one and the same. Write in your journal about your thoughts and feelings on this topic.

3

Understanding Your Emotions

There can be no transforming of darkness into light and of apathy into movement without emotion.

—Carl Gustav Jung

*M*ost of the people I've worked with who are contemplating divorce are exhausted. Figuring out what actions to take next while riding the emotional roller coaster of uncertainty is incredibly draining. The predominant emotions you will likely experience in this important decision-making process are fear, helplessness, confusion, sadness, and anger—especially early on. It's normal for all of these different feelings, as well as many others, to be elicited when you are trying to sort out marital problems and determine whether or not your relationship with your spouse can work out.

This chapter will focus on helping you understand the emotions you may experience and learn how you can have more control over these feelings. When you don't feel overrun by your emotions, you can make decisions from a more solid place and consequently make better decisions.

In a group session one evening, Missy eloquently described her self-observations and why it was important for her to get a handle on her emotions. She said, "One minute I feel so guilty about contemplating leaving that I think, if I do file, I should just give him everything. But then, in a split second he can make me so mad that I want to serve him with divorce papers right then and there, and make him pay through the teeth forever!"

If Missy had acted from either of these extreme emotions, she would not have been happy later, nor would she have really gotten what she wanted, which was separation from her husband and peace in her life. Because she sought and received emotional support, Missy was eventually able to come to the decision to leave her marriage in an amicable way, from a solid place, not a reactionary one.

Another woman who took my Contemplating Divorce workshop told me she was trying to avoid her usual pattern of "Ready, fire, aim!" She correctly observed that her compulsiveness had taken her from many bad situations into many worse ones, and she wanted to do everything in her power to focus on her true needs instead of merely lashing out in anger while deciding whether or not to stay in her marriage.

There are many things in life that we are taught to handle solo, but deciding whether to stay married or get a divorce is not something I recommend that you try to figure out alone.

The Grief Progression

When contemplating divorce, you will likely experience a series of different emotions along what I call the "grief progression." Based on Elisabeth Kübler-Ross's stages of grief (1969, 38–112), this progression is a compilation of many different responses I have witnessed my clients undergo.

While there are certain commonalities to all grieving processes, each person has a different experience of grief and loss from change. Figure 2 is intended as a guide to help you understand what you have already gone through, where you are currently in your process, and what feelings you might encounter as you continue assessing where you are headed in your marriage.

At this point, you already may have completed at least one cycle of grieving, which often accompanies the initial realization that your spouse is not the person you hoped he or she was or would become. Regardless of the outcome of this decision-making process, you will likely experience more cycles of grief as you continue through it.

This is not necessarily a linear process, so your emotions may bounce you from one stage to another, or you might even feel as if you're in two stages at the same time. Because you will experience this same cycle on many levels at different stages in your contemplation process, I suggest that you refer back to this grief progression often. You may find it comforting, especially at times when you question yourself the most.

Phase 1: Initial Loss

You may have felt a sense of being stunned when you got the first real inkling that your spouse was not who you thought or hoped he or she was, or that the marriage was not what you hoped it would be. The initial feelings can be shock, disbelief, and numbness.

It's not uncommon to try to shut down the shock that comes with grief and loss. This shutting down is what leads to disbelieving or denying what is happening, and possibly even becoming numb. You may effectively say to yourself, "This can't be real" or "If I don't see it, maybe it will go away!" These instinctual reactions attempt to protect you by helping you avoid your current unpleasant reality.

Phase 2: Protest

When you began to open up to the idea that you might not be with your spouse forever after all, you may have tried to negate your feelings by telling yourself that you were imagining things or were simply focusing too much on your spouse's negative aspects. You may not have wanted to let go of your dream of living happily ever after. You may have wished it could all be different and that circumstances would change so that you wouldn't have to. It has likely made you frustrated and sad, and even made you angry that you couldn't get back the innocence or harmony that your marriage once enjoyed.

Your friends and family may have perpetuated your denial by telling you to ignore your feelings and stop being so picky, or, not knowing what you have been through up to this point, that it's just a passing phase.

Your response to such notions may be anger, fear, or both. You may feel as if you are on an emotional roller coaster, spending your energy

FIGURE 2: THE GRIEF PROGRESSION

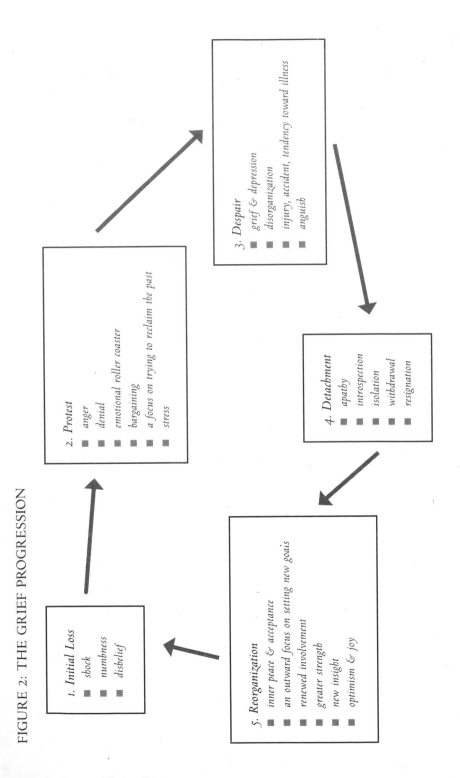

1. *Initial Loss*
   ▪ *shock*
   ▪ *numbness*
   ▪ *disbelief*

2. *Protest*
   ▪ *anger*
   ▪ *denial*
   ▪ *emotional roller coaster*
   ▪ *bargaining*
   ▪ *a focus on trying to reclaim the past*
   ▪ *stress*

3. *Despair*
   ▪ *grief & depression*
   ▪ *disorganization*
   ▪ *injury, accident, tendency toward illness*
   ▪ *anguish*

4. *Detachment*
   ▪ *apathy*
   ▪ *introspection*
   ▪ *isolation*
   ▪ *withdrawal*
   ▪ *resignation*

5. *Reorganization*
   ▪ *inner peace & acceptance*
   ▪ *an outward focus on setting new goals*
   ▪ *renewed involvement*
   ▪ *greater strength*
   ▪ *new insight*
   ▪ *optimism & joy*

bargaining with your spouse or struggling to reclaim the past. Because the nature of this phase is to protest, it is by far the most exhausting phase of the grief progression, causing you to expend great amounts of energy fighting reality and trying to stop feeling the negative emotions.

Phase 3: Despair

In the despair phase, you've reached a deeper level of pain and realized that you can no longer stay in the unhealthy or unfulfilling environment. This stage moves you further into sadness, which, more than any other emotion, may make you feel out of control. However, this sadness absolutely needs acknowledging, regardless of your final decision about whether to stay married or get divorced. You are grieving the loss of the idea of whom you thought you were married to or the dreams your marriage represented to you.

Following your initial sadness, your thoughts may be something like this: "It really *is* as bad as I feared. I've tried everything I know to work on the relationship and improve things between us, but I can't force change. I'm deeply saddened and angry that my partner isn't acting like a partner and that this relationship is not as I would have it be."

You're probably restless, preoccupied with grief, and uncertain what to do next. You may even feel as if your world were falling apart. Your inability to make the situation any better may make you feel disempowered and hopeless. Adding sadness to the difficult emotions of anger, restlessness, uncertainty, and hopelessness that you were already experiencing can be particularly draining.

At this stage in the grief progression, because you are so deeply entrenched in trying to figure out the next steps, you will not be fully present. You may be particularly vulnerable to injuries, illnesses, and accidents from your inability to focus on the current moment.

Phase 4: Detachment

The principal reaction you will experience in the detachment phase is withdrawal from normal social contact and interaction with others. This is a time to go within and put your needs above those of everyone else around you.

Prior to this phase, you may have spent an inordinate amount of energy trying to change your spouse or some aspect of your situation. In this detachment phase, in essence, you resign yourself to the fact that you cannot control anyone but yourself, so you stop caring so much and focusing on people and things outside yourself.

Such detachment is a normal and healthy response to this type of situation. One benefit of this coping mechanism is that you conserve your energy. It is a form of self-preservation in the sense that continuing to work too hard or care too much about a situation would surely make you burn out. Instead, you begin to go within and assess how you can meet your own needs instead of trying to get others to meet or understand your needs.

Those close to you may resist your growth, but when you disengage from unhealthy people or dynamics, and instead focus on what you *can* change, you gain strength. You will need this strength to move into the next phase, which entails setting new goals for yourself. In all likelihood, once you are on the other side of that phase, you will resume closer-to-normal interactions with others.

Phase 5: Reorganization

Although I mentioned that this grief progression is not necessarily a linear cycle, the reorganization phase—characterized by the more positive emotions of happiness, inner peace and acceptance, and optimism and joy—can't fully occur unless you have passed through the earlier phases. It makes sense that you won't begin to feel good again until you either accept your current reality as it is or make a firm decision to create the necessary changes to get where you want to be. The happiness you may experience here will be the springboard into the next chapter of your life.

Projecting into the future is required at this stage, as you start planning what's next, with or without your spouse. As a couple, you either move on together and work on the marital issues, or split up and begin your new lives as single individuals.

In either case, you will have a renewed excitement for life, new insights, and increased strength; you'll feel that you have something to look forward to. Unlike the previous stages of the grief progression, when your negative emotions drain you, these new, positive emotions will propel you forward with new energy.

As much as you may want to, you can't skip any of the five stages of the grief progression. You may certainly have your own version of each phase, but you will have to pass through each experience.

The more you can surrender to experiencing the emotions accompanying the grief progression, the smoother your divorce-contemplation process will go. Most people compound their difficult emotions by creating an added story line. The story, or meaning, you give the event then causes a whole new set of potentially detrimental emotions, because all such emotions require energy, which explains the exhaustion you experience when you're in a highly emotional state. This second set of emotions further saps your time, energy, and resources to process the feelings, but because these additional emotions are based on an invented story line, the energy you use to feel them is wasted.

My suggestion that you feel some feelings while reining in others may seem contradictory, but read on. I will expand more on this idea and clarify it later in this chapter in the subsection titled "Managing Your Emotions."

To learn more about the grief progression, let's look at the following examples, which demonstrate how the progression shows up in the lives of people contemplating divorce, regardless of whether or not they wind up divorcing. The first example is about a couple who ends up separating, but the second stays together.

■ Case Example: Gabriela and Matthew's Story

When she came out of denying her husband's alcoholism, Gabriela's heart sank. She said she felt as if someone had pulled the plug from the outlet of her spirit. To say that she was numb would've been an understatement; Gabriela couldn't think, feel, or act.

This frozen state lasted for a couple of weeks before the realities of her dismal options came to the surface: stay with an unpredictable, abusive alcoholic, or leave. She found herself overwhelmed with anger that she married an alcoholic without seeing the warning signs, that he chose alcohol over her and the kids and refused to get treatment, and even that she couldn't just accept his addiction and abusive behavior and live with it as the people in Al-Anon seemed to do.

Gabriela's anger propelled her into action and self-care. Along with her therapy with me, she began reading books that deepened her understanding of the 12-step program and the role of her Al-Anon sponsor, and was doing all she could to work on becoming a better person and partner.

She wasn't sure what would happen with her marriage but was determined to improve herself so that if she did stay, she would be stronger and healthier; and if she left, and dated again in the future, she would make better choices.

As Gabriela began to feel better, much to her dismay, Matthew behaved worse. He became less functional and more abusive. Although every fiber in her being told her, "You don't divorce, no matter what," she realized that she couldn't change her husband and, despite her tremendous love for him, couldn't get him sober or help him recover. It broke Gabriela's heart. She felt as if she had to make the decision to cut off her best friend, the father of her children, and a wonderful person, or allow herself to continue to be mistreated. Neither choice was good or easy, but ultimately, as she said, she "voted for" herself.

When she made the choice to stop trying to push the square peg into the round hole, Gabriela stopped focusing so much on Matthew and, in turn, felt a tremendous weight removed from her shoulders. She felt even lighter and freer when Matthew, who agreed that he should be the one to leave, moved out.

Gabriela now had her own space and, although she felt a sense of relief, was surprised to find that Matthew's moving out set her back again into the second and third phases of grief progression: protest and despair. This actually happened several times.

As she moved forward and started feeling better, she encountered events that sent her backwards in the progression, such as running into someone and having to explain her marital situation, or discovering that something around the house needed fixing. Despite my conveying to her that it was a normal and expected part of the process, Gabriela couldn't get used to her emotions bouncing around, so this always surprised her.

■ Case Example: Jim and Michele's Story

Jim and Michele had both been married once before, and Michele had two children, ages eight and ten. Almost immediately after getting married, Jim was surprised to find himself faced with a tough situation.

Michele seemed to change the minute she and Jim returned from their honeymoon in the way she treated her children, Anna and Leigh. She had been very attentive to Jim prior to tying the knot but now seemed less interested in him and instead gave almost all of her time and attention to her two girls.

It was a surreal experience for Jim, which he had no idea how to handle at first. Since he suspected he was possibly just feeling insecure, he decided to say nothing until he was sure this shift of attention had indeed occurred.

Despite the fact that Jim did all he could to give Michele the benefit of the doubt and deny his own needs, he could no longer ignore his feelings. He discussed with Michele his concern that she might not be as "into him" as when they had dated. Michele became somewhat defensive and told Jim that he was just imagining things. Jim's asking Michele about her feelings actually put an overt strain on their new marriage.

Jim was so angered by his feelings of being dismissed that he didn't know what to do. He felt as if he had just made a huge mistake, and suspected that Michele might be using him to provide financial support for her and her daughters. He wished he had seen this coming and felt absolutely duped.

As time went on, Jim became quite resigned to feeling like the fifth wheel. He felt that he and Michele got along fine as long as he didn't bring up his need to spend more time with her. Michele continued giving the majority of her attention to her daughters, and Jim just made the best of it.

The marriage wasn't awful, but Jim just didn't feel like a part of this new family. He started to consider separating from Michele, since he felt like an outsider to her and her daughters when they were all together. Jim became more and more detached from the marriage. One day, he worked up the nerve to tell Michele that he was considering leaving because he felt more alone now than before they had met.

. Michele was absolutely stunned. Even though Jim thought he had expressed his need for more of her attention early in the marriage, Michele didn't know what Jim was talking about. She hadn't meant to shut Jim out and honestly didn't see things the same way he did. She had no idea how important this issue was for him. Michele asked Jim what he needed from her to stay, and he responded that he needed more alone time with her than they currently had.

Michele was able to respond in a way that made Jim feel acknowledged. Once or twice a week, they went out together, just the two of them without the girls. Jim felt that the relationship was back on track, and although he had seriously considered leaving, they were able to work through this issue so that he felt good about staying in the marriage. Michele seemed happier with the changes too.

The truth is, they loved each other a great deal and got along well. Focusing on the kids was simply an unconscious habit that Michele had slipped into (a pattern that she later realized had contributed to the demise of her first marriage). Once she recognized this, she was able to change her old habits and increase her participation in the marital relationship.

In both examples, the spouse who needed the relationship to change went through all the stages of the grief progression. Both Gabriela and Jim experienced the initial loss of the individuals they married, once they noticed the undesirable behavior in their spouses. They both went through their own versions of denial and bargaining, by pretending the situation was better than it was or trying to figure out how to improve things. Then, each moved into a deeper sadness over the inability to change the relationship, which led to a resignation that this was indeed the reality, and with that, both became willing to let go of their marriages. Finally, an inner reorganization occurred, which for Gabriela meant moving on without her husband and for Jim meant a renewed involvement in the marital relationship.

Exercise: Your Grieving Process

Knowing where you are in the grief progression can be like looking at the map of a mall and finding the "You are here" notification. You become better oriented and gain a better sense of where you are headed. This exercise will help you do just that. As a reminder, phases 1 through 5 of the grief progression are:

1. Initial Loss   4. Detachment

2. Protest   5. Reorganization

3. Despair

Answering the following questions will help you identify what your grieving experience has been so far:

1. What phase of the grief progression are you currently in?

2. What events in your marriage do you believe have brought you to this stage?

3. What other phases have you experienced?

4. Briefly describe each stage of the grief progression that you have experienced to this point. Examples: Initial loss—I felt wracked with fear all the time and had no idea which way to turn; protest—every morning, I woke up with a sense of dread that this was my reality.

5. How do you, or did you, cope with your discomfort at each stage in the grief progression?

Here are examples of questions to answer at each phase:

Initial loss (shock)—When you first felt shock that your spouse might not be the perfect mate, what did you do or say?

Protest (anger or fear)—When you first felt angry at your spouse for not being the person you had hoped he or she would be, did you express your anger to your spouse or hold it in?

Despair (sadness)—When you have felt sadness over losing your dream of the ideal relationship with your spouse, how have you handled that sadness?

Detachment (apathy)—When you have felt detached, have you been more emotionally and physically distant from your spouse?

Reorganization (happiness)—Does the thought of creating a happy and fulfilling life for yourself cause you to feel guilty?

If you have any other thoughts about your grieving process, I encourage you to write about them in your journal. You can continue to use this exercise as a reference point if you begin to feel lost or overwhelmed in your grieving process.

Weathering the Emotional Storm

Being in the midst of such an emotional storm, you might be surprised to learn that you can actually control how long your process lasts and how bad you feel. As I mentioned in the last section, you won't be able to skip the grieving process, but you can experience your emotions, keep them in check, and keep them from taking over your entire life by not altering the real story with what you might be tempted to add to the mix.

The key is to increase your understanding of emotions—what they are and how they operate—by knowing the meaning you give to events and gaining a higher tolerance for discomfort. In the next few subsections, you will learn the skills you need to manage your emotions.

Avoiding Bad Feelings

Most of us believe that we shouldn't have negative emotions, so when a challenging event comes up in our lives that makes us feel bad, mad, or sad, we often think there is something wrong with us. We try to keep these uncomfortable feelings in a little box in the corner or hack them out of our experience altogether in any number of ways, such as staying busy, numbing out, becoming consumed by an addiction, or buying toys and material possessions. We get out of or into a relationship, find a new job, or make up stories to get a sense of control over what's happening. Let's see how this manifests.

■ *Case Example:* Ron and Cheryl's Story

It took Ron four years to realize that he was unhappy in his marriage. For a long time, he assumed it was residual stress from his job that made him ornery with his wife, Cheryl.

Ron felt unhappy on a daily basis but expended a lot of energy shooing away the feelings by telling himself to stop complaining, or justifying his feelings by reflecting that work wasn't supposed to be enjoyable because it was just a means to an end. It wasn't until Ron changed jobs that he realized his melancholy mood might have more to do with his relationship than his career.

This was the point at which Ron decided to get into therapy to see if he could "chase away these negative feelings that dog me every day." I explained that he would benefit by exploring the feelings, not getting rid of them. At first he firmly resisted the idea but eventually came to understand its wisdom.

We worked together for close to six months before he was able to uncover that what bothered him was that he didn't like how he felt about himself when Cheryl was around. He found her subtle, and sometimes not-so-subtle, put-downs wearing.

He remembered that his father had treated him in much the same way, making him feel small and self-doubtful so that he could totally control Ron. By exploring this dynamic, Ron got in touch with some very deep sadness that he had tried to squelch for over thirty years. This discovery, as well as working to change the beliefs he held about himself, helped

Ron stand up to Cheryl, which in turn helped him heal the unresolved sadness and anger toward his father, who had died many years earlier.

Ron's first instinct had been to stop experiencing his negative emotions because they made him uncomfortable. For a while, he seriously considered asking Cheryl for a divorce, just to make the feelings go away. He was so resistant to dealing with the true cause of his feelings that divorce actually seemed like an easier option.

But if Ron had not confronted these underlying feelings, he wouldn't have uncovered an unconscious thought pattern that he had internalized from his father, which continued to keep him feeling small and unhappy. He could have gotten away from his wife but probably would have repeated the pattern somewhere else in his life, with a boss, a neighbor, a friend, or in another romantic relationship.

In this case, Ron was able to confront Cheryl, who recognized that her behavior was unacceptable, and they were able to work out their marital problems in a mature, healthy way.

Managing Your Emotions

Our emotions are not like physical sensations wherein there is a predictable response to a particular stimulus. When you get too close to a fire, you feel pain; or when you sink into a nice warm bath, you feel relaxed.

The majority of our emotions are filtered through our thoughts, which have been shaped more by our past experiences than by the present event we are responding to. Since we all have different backgrounds, our emotional responses will be less consistent from person to person than our physical reactions. So, how does this work and how do feelings get formed?

First, there has to be an event. Usually, we have an initial split-second unfiltered reaction to what happened. Next, we assign the event a meaning. This meaning or thought is essentially a filter that determines the next level of feelings (filtered feelings) about the event. Finally, we take an action that reflects how we feel about ourselves or about the event.

The following flow chart demonstrates how this dynamic works:

FIGURE 3: HOW FEELINGS GET FILTERED

EVENT ➜ UNFILTERED ➜ THOUGHT ➜ FILTERED ➜ ACTION
FEELING   FILTERS   FEELING

Since you have your own unique experiences and vantage point on life, you may react differently than other people to exactly the same event. For example, if you were told you had just won an all-expense-paid trip around the world, your very first reaction would be something like surprise. Then, depending on what significance such a trip has, there may be a variety of responses: you might be ecstatic while your spouse might go right into feeling resistance or dread, but had your sister won, she might be apathetic about it and give the trip away to a friend. So there's one event with three different people and three very distinct reactions.

What I hope you come away with after reading this subsection is that you can always choose how to interpret the events in your life. Your feelings about an event are one thing; how you interpret them is quite another. But changing your interpretation changes the way you feel and, ultimately, how you act and react to situations.

■ *Case Example:* Phyllis and Ricky, and Rachael and Max's Story

Phyllis and Rachael grew up together as best friends in a small town in New England. Coincidentally, they ended up going to the same college, where both women met the men who would become their husbands. These women had a great deal in common, but something happened that highlighted how differently each viewed marriage.

About fifteen years into their marriage, Phyllis's husband, Ricky, started having an affair. Initially, Phyllis was upset but, within a very short amount of time, concluded that all men have affairs, and as long as he was discreet and didn't let it impact the marriage, she could turn a blind eye. She knew that her mother had the same philosophy about men, and it just seemed to be the natural course of events in a marriage.

In contrast, two years later, Rachael's husband, Max, had an affair with his office assistant. Rachael was so upset and felt so betrayed that she immediately kicked him out of the house and filed for divorce as soon as she could. There were no second chances. An affair marked the end of the marriage for her, whereas with her good friend, it just marked a new phase of the marriage.

Phyllis expected her husband to have an affair and assumed it was part of the marriage package. When he did find a lover, it wasn't an event that caused the marriage to end. On the other hand, Rachael expected that her husband would never cheat on her and that this type of behavior was 100 percent unacceptable, so when he did cheat, she had zero tolerance.

Each woman gave a completely different meaning to her husband's cheating, based on prior life experience. The different meanings they attributed to the same action determined their different feelings and responses to it.

How Thought Habits Create Feeling Habits

The meaning you associate with events is directly related to your experience and beliefs about yourself and the world around you. If you are a generally confident person, your perspective will usually be that the glass is half full. If you lack self-esteem, you will likely see the glass as half empty. When in a good mood, you are less likely to take it personally when someone is rude to you, but when in a bad place emotionally, you will be more sensitive and may even feel as if the world is out to get you.

While current circumstances color your view, much of your current perspective on life is based on what you learned when you were young. You unknowingly developed ways of thinking that eventually became habits. Today, as an adult, your thoughts are so preprogrammed and ingrained that you probably aren't even aware of their presence most of the time.

It's not unlike learning to drive. When you first got into a car, placing the key in the ignition; putting the vehicle in drive; or turning on the radio, windshield wipers, or heat was very mechanical. As you drove, you had to focus intently on where everything was located, while holding the steering wheel straight.

Once you've driven for many years, you can jump into the car, talk on the cell phone, drink your coffee, turn on the air-conditioning, and get to where you're going seemingly without much thought.

When you think the same types of thoughts over and over, you can buy into them without even realizing that they are running the show and determining how you experience life. The lens through which you view everything feels so accurate and natural that, if you are like most of us, you are tempted to assume that everyone sees the world the same way you do.

When you start your day each morning, do you have a thought habit?—something you tell yourself about how the day will go, how well you like or dislike what you are doing, or how you feel in general? My guess is that you do, and more than likely, you and your spouse have developed ways of acting and reacting to each other that you don't think twice about.

The first step in changing your thoughts is to become aware that they are there. By developing the skill of recognizing the thoughts that serve as your filter, you will have a more open mind to others' reactions and the ability to choose how you want to react.

Exercise: Changing Your Thought Habits

This exercise is designed to help you put into practice the concepts outlined in this chapter. Understanding that others may see things drastically differently than you do, and why that is so, may help change limiting beliefs you didn't even know you had.

This series of questions can be applied to any and all incidents in which your emotions got the best of you or there was an outdated thought pattern that you'd like to change.

1. Write about a time in your life when someone close to you (not necessarily your spouse) had a completely different reaction to an event than you did, or than you thought they should. What did you think about this person's response? Did you try to talk the person out of his or her feelings or perceptions? Did a disagreement ensue? Were either of you able to see the other's perspective, or did you simply agree to disagree?

2. Write about a thought habit that you would like to change about either yourself or the world around you. Some examples might be: "I will never be as successful as my brother" or "I have nothing to offer." How did this thought get planted in your mind?

3. Write a new affirming thought that counteracts the old thought habit. Some examples might be: "I am more and more successful every day" or "Success comes to me easily and effortlessly."

4. Write about an unconscious pattern of acting and reacting that you and your spouse have experienced over and over that you wish were different.

5. What can you do to change this pattern?

Once you begin to consistently change your thought habits (which usually takes lots of practice), you will see that many other changes follow. You will see the world in a new way and react differently, and people will treat you differently.

RESPONDING DIFFERENTLY TO THOUGHTS AND FEELINGS

Your beliefs about yourself and the world play a major role in how you feel about yourself, your spouse, and your relationship. While the thoughts behind these beliefs are relatively firmly planted in your mind, they are nothing more than a culmination of what you have learned about yourself, and can be replaced with new thoughts and beliefs. In turn, this will alter your reactions to life's situations.

The meaning you give to events can change when you make a concerted effort to assign a new interpretation to, or get new information about, the events. This was illustrated in Ron and Cheryl's story, in which Ron was able to uncover old ways of thinking about himself, change these thoughts, and thereby improve his relationship.

Let's look again at Phyllis and Ricky's story, specifically at Phyllis's reaction to Ricky's affair fifteen years ago. She was relatively accepting of his behavior because she believed that this was simply what all married men did. But after taking part in a relationship insight group and some self-improvement seminars, Phyllis was introduced to many men who did not, and would not, cheat on their wives. In addition, she consulted a male therapist for a while, who assured her that while unfaithful men may have been *her* norm, it was not necessarily *the* norm. This was eye opening for her.

The final shifting point for Phyllis was her friend Rachael's reaction of not condoning her own husband Max's cheating. By being exposed to a wider range of possibilities, Phyllis was influenced by new information and subsequently changed her viewpoint. This enabled her to go from believing that a cheating husband was a fact of life to feeling that she deserved a husband she could trust. Phyllis stopped allowing Ricky to have extramarital affairs.

In this particular situation, Phyllis's husband respected her wishes. He put an end to his extramarital affair, and they have remained married. Both would tell you that it took a lot of work from each of them, but this couple wanted to stay married more than they wanted to divorce, so they did what it took to save the marriage.

We can see from Phyllis and Ricky's story that feelings can change. Both had to make some changes in their views on life and matrimony to stay married.

Exercise: Changing Your Responses

This exercise will help you identify one or more ways in which your behavior changed when you changed the thoughts through which you filtered your feelings.

1. Think of a behavior your spouse exhibits that has different meaning for you now than it used to. How has your reaction to this behavior changed? (See examples before filling in.)

Behavior	Your Old Response	Your Newer Response
My husband smokes pot.	*I don't care. I look the other way. I make excuses for him.*	*I don't condone it and don't cover for his mistakes anymore.*
I always have to ask my spouse to clean the kitchen.	*I kept expecting her to do the dishes and took it as a personal affront that she didn't do them.*	*I understand that my spouse doesn't take care of a lot of things, and it is not meant to hurt me when she lets things go.*

Behavior	Your Old Response	Your Newer Response
_____	_____	_____
_____	_____	_____

2. Write about what has shifted for you, your spouse, or your relationship that you believe has caused or contributed to the change in your response.

Opening your mind to other possibilities takes practice but is quite rewarding. Choosing a new reaction to a situation is not only incredibly empowering to you, but those around you also benefit.

All Emotions Are Not Created Equal

At the beginning of this chapter, I mentioned that there are certain emotions you will want to express and others that you will want to rein in. This is because some types of emotions will be constructive to getting through your process, whereas other types will be destructive. At this point, you are probably wondering why all emotions aren't equal. How can some be constructive and others be destructive?

The way I explain it to my clients is that there are two different types of emotions: the immediate feelings you get from the actual life event (unfiltered), and those you get from the story you make up about the event (filtered). Even though the actual feelings may be the same (for example, sadness, anger, or fear), the important difference is the cause of the feelings. It's one thing to be sad because someone you love dies (unfiltered emotion), but it's another type of sadness to go on to imagine what life would be like if all your friends were to die (filtered emotion).

The unfiltered feelings are constructive in that they occur in response to a real event and are about the present moment. You benefit from acknowledging these emotions and allowing yourself to feel them. When you sit with these emotions, they eventually pass.

Filtered emotions are the ones that serve no purpose other than to alter your mood and take you out of the present moment. These can be negative or positive fantasies about the future, as well as dreamy reminiscences or regrets about the past. They can be over- or underreactions to a situation based on beliefs about yourself, such as "I'll never find a man to love me" or "I'm not worthy of being truly happy." Clearly, you don't benefit from these filtered feelings, since they are based on fear, a bad mood, or low self-esteem rather than actual facts. The more you sit with these feelings, the worse you feel, and because these feelings don't stop until you stop the thoughts that create them, they can go on indefinitely.

UNFILTERED VS. FILTERED FEELINGS

Let's look back again at Ron and Cheryl's story to better understand unfiltered versus filtered emotions. Ron felt a deep-seated sadness from being hurt by his father, which carried over into his relationship with his wife Cheryl. This unfiltered feeling made Ron feel uncomfortable and out of control, so he developed thought filters to feel in control. The thought filters created a different set of emotions, which in turn impacted whom he gravitated toward and raised his tolerance for unacceptable treatment from others.

If we were to diagram Ron's filtering process, it would look like this:

FIGURE 4: THOUGHT-FILTERING PROCESS

EVENT → Ron's father abused Ron emotionally.

UNFILTERED FEELING → Ron felt very sad.

THOUGHT FILTERS → Ron began to put himself down and told himself he was worthless.

FILTERED FEELING → Ron then felt ashamed, bad, stupid, and wrong.

ACTION → Ron stayed in situations that matched and perpetuated his negative feelings about himself.

Unfiltered emotions normally relay necessary information for you to heal from the original event. These feelings can actually help move you to a better place in your life, but because they can be scary or uncomfortable, or make you feel out of control, you may prefer to avoid them. Most people want to escape these emotions as soon as possible to regain a sense of control over their lives.

But if you ignore or squelch these unfiltered feelings, you may miss the important messages they would normally provide. Not only that, but you will probably continue to attract people and situations that will re-create the very scenario you wish to avoid. A later subsection in this chapter, "Uncovering Your Unfiltered Emotions," outlines how to acknowledge these feelings and learn from them.

Filtered emotions disguise themselves as helpful, but in reality they are anything but. In fact, they can take an average situation and spin it so far out of proportion that you are rendered useless. What I find most ironic about this is that we use these filters to help us feel more in control by finding the reasons why something occurred. This is a function of the human brain and one of the more fascinating aspects that separates us from lower species. Unfortunately, it doesn't always serve us well.

While unfiltered feelings can be intense due to their raw nature, filtered feelings are based on a story you have *created*, not on something that actually happened. You actually waste valuable energy by reacting to something imaginary. Ron spent a lot more time and energy telling himself he was bad and wrong for having his feelings than he did uncovering why he was unhappy or trying to heal his deep sadness.

Exercise: How Do You Really Feel?

This exercise can help you increase your awareness about your unfiltered feelings, what particular thought filter you run the feelings through, and what filtered feeling you end up with as a result.

1. Think of a time in the past few months when you felt upset or stressed about something, and write about it using the format that follows:

EVENT → UNFILTERED → THOUGHT → FILTERED → ACTION
          FEELING   FILTERS   FEELING

| What happened? | What was your initial feeling? | What meaning did you give the event? | How did that make you feel? | What did you do? |

Don't be surprised if you can't remember your initial feelings in response to an event. These reactions can occur so spontaneously and quickly that you don't even notice or remember them. In addition, there are often events that occurred when you were very young that have impacted you, but due to your young age and developmental limitations at the time, you won't be able to remember your unfiltered response.

An example one woman gave me involved tracing feelings of inherent inadequacy resulting from having been hit by her mother before age four. She doesn't remember being hit, but her mother later told her that, prior to learning that hitting was child abuse, she used to spank the daughter's bottom whenever the daughter did something her mom considered wrong. Her mother told her that the daughter went into crying jags lasting for close to an hour after being spanked. This woman deduced that she must have internalized a deep sense that she was bad because her mother hit her, even though she doesn't remember clearly thinking those thoughts.

2. Can you see how you arrived at your filtered feeling and how this filtered feeling impacted what action you then took? How does knowing this help you?

It may be useful to write down other actions you might have taken instead of the one you took in this situation. This isn't meant to create judgment; rather, the idea is to open your mind to the notion that you always have a choice in what story you tell yourself, and thus how you feel and what action you take.

NORMAL EMOTIONAL RESPONSES

With unfiltered emotions, there may be some variations on different people's emotional responses to any one occurrence. However, certain feelings are considered "normal," in that most people having a similar experience will feel similar feelings in response. For example, it's considered normal to feel sad when someone close to you dies, angry over a betrayal, or excited about a new job opportunity.

When you ignore your unfiltered feelings, they grow. A good analogy is a child tugging at the sleeve of an adult. If the child is ignored or told to be quiet, what usually happens? He or she usually starts to scream or cry and becomes more demanding, not less. Acting much like a child, the unfiltered emotion that needs our attention won't go away until it is acknowledged.

There are only six unfiltered emotions: happiness, sadness, anger, surprise, fear, and disgust (Satterfield 2007). These can also be filtered feelings, but no other emotions are considered to be unfiltered besides these six. Often, we have little or no sense of control over these unfiltered emotions, so they make us feel vulnerable, even the positive one.

Most of us try to cover up these feelings, push them away, or somehow gain control over them. We do this by inventing stories about the impact of the events on our lives. If we can think of all possible worst-case scenarios, in the off chance that they ever materialize, we will know what to expect and will already have felt the feelings that go with the event. We presume that nothing can catch us off guard or hurt us.

Because they are based on each person's experience and story, filtered emotions offer a wider range of possible feelings than unfiltered ones. Because we all have different experiences, others' reactions can really surprise us, especially when they differ much from our own responses.

Our stories create a whole new set of emotions, but because we are the ones to "write" them, we feel less vulnerable and more in control of our feelings. I call these "filtered emotions" because they are in direct response to the story and *indirect* response to the event.

Allowing yourself to feel your filtered emotions doesn't help your situation, because they distract you from the actual event, whereas letting yourself feel the unfiltered emotions forces you to deal with what is real.

We always have the option of whether or not to entertain these filtered emotions. We're just not always aware that we have this choice. One woman I worked with on distinguishing filtered from unfiltered emotions came to a session one day feeling elated, because she had finally been able to stop some filtered emotions from running her life. She said that one night during the week prior to our meeting, while nodding off to sleep she began to think of her house, which she had been forced to lease because of her divorce.

She was concerned about finding a good tenant, which is normal, but within minutes she found herself completely wound up over how hard it would be to find one: It was the wrong time of year to lease. Would someone be able to pay what she needed? What if she got a difficult tenant as had happened once before? And on and on and on.

Realizing that she was creating her own anxiety by anticipating challenges that hadn't yet happened, she actually said out loud to herself, "No! I'm not going there." She refused to let herself obsess about these possible negative scenarios any longer and soon fell asleep.

Any time she started thinking about how hard it might be to get a new tenant, she replaced the worry with a positive thought instead, such as "I only need to find one right tenant." When the time actually came to find a new tenant, she found the most perfect couple right away, and her house was only empty for two weeks. She would have lost sleep over nothing. Instead, she put her energy into fixing up the house and taking care of the other matters in her life that needed attention.

The key to improving your process will be to develop the skill of identifying when you feel anger, sorrow, joy, or fear from the actual event, versus when you feel filtered emotions from the story you are telling yourself.

When you find yourself deeply entrenched in your emotions, stop in your tracks and ask yourself first *what* you feel and then *why* you feel that emotion. For example, did something just happen to make you feel this way, or have you made up a story that made you feel mad, sad, or scared?

Aside from deciphering whether your feeling is based on something that just happened or on a story you told yourself about it, another revealing factor that can help you distinguish one type of emotion from the other is the complexity of the emotion. The simpler the emotion, the more likely it is to be an unfiltered emotion.

UNCOVERING YOUR UNFILTERED EMOTIONS

Perhaps you have so many filters in place and are focused so intently on listening to your filtered stories that you can't believe there ever *was* an original unfiltered emotion; never mind *uncovering* it. How can you get to where you can understand that original feeling?

One of the tricks that I have used when feeling particularly stuck is to write down the event and then write about how I feel now:

EVENT →   My car was stolen.

FILTERED FEELINGS →   Incredibly violated, scared, angry, financially insecure, nostalgic

I can't remember what my initial reaction was, but as I observe my filtered thoughts, I can start asking questions about each feeling, which will begin to uncover the thought filters.

Filtered Feeling	Thought Filter
Why do I feel violated?	Someone went into my car without my permission. They took it, and I need it.

Why do I feel scared?	I'm afraid that this person will hurt me. I'm afraid of all the possible ramifications this will have.
Why do I feel angry?	It's not okay with me that someone took my car! That's selfish and wrong of them. That person was only thinking of himself. I don't have the time or money to deal with this right now. I was only gone for one hour. I feel disempowered now.
Why do I feel financially insecure?	This is going to cost me lots of money. I don't have the money to get a new car, and insurance won't give me enough to get a decent replacement.
Why do I feel nostalgic?	I loved that car. My grandmother gave it to me, and it was my first car.

I can now look at the six unfiltered emotions—mad, sad, glad, scared, disgusted, and surprised—and try to figure out which ones apply to my situation:

Filtered Feeling	Thought Filter	Unfiltered Feeling
Why do I feel violated?	Someone went into my car without my permission. They took it, and I need it.	surprised, disgusted
Why do I feel scared?	I'm afraid that this person will hurt me. I'm afraid of all the ramifications.	scared

Filtered Feeling	Thought Filter	Unfiltered Feeling
Why do I feel angry?	It's not okay with me that someone took my car! That's selfish and wrong of them. That person was only thinking of himself. I don't have the time or money to deal with this right now. I feel disempowered.	mad, disgusted, and scared
Why do I feel financially insecure?	This is going to cost me lots of money. I don't have the money to get a new car, and insurance won't give me enough.	scared
Why do I feel nostalgic?	I loved that car. My grandmother gave it to me, and it was my first car.	sad

The unfiltered emotions are surprised, disgusted, scared, mad, and sad. The filtered emotions are violated, scared, angry, insecure, and nostalgic. You can see from this example how much more complex the filtered emotions often are, even though some of the filtered and unfiltered emotions are the same.

In the event that you can't uncover your unfiltered emotions even after doing this exercise, think about how you believe most people would feel if they had just found out their cars was stolen. Sometimes it's easier to depersonalize the event to understand it better.

Discovering your unfiltered emotions is a skill to be learned and practiced.

CONTROLLING YOUR FILTERED EMOTIONS

Once you have your stories down on paper, you can begin to see whether or not they are true stories. By dissecting the emotions you feel when contemplating whether or not to end your marriage, the stories will become particularly evident. For example, "When I think about getting divorced, I feel scared."

Fear is a normal emotion that comes up for most, if not all, divorcing people. It's not enough to look at the feeling to know whether it is a filtered or unfiltered emotion. You must ask *why* you feel that particular emotion.

I feel scared because...

1. I will be all alone.   T or F

2. I won't have anyone to talk to about my day.   T or F

3. I don't know what divorce entails.   T or F

4. I will be a bag lady on the streets.   T or F

5. No one will ever love me again.   T or F

6. I'm too old to date.   T or F

Obviously, depending on how you answer the question, you will see whether the fears are based on the truth, an exaggeration, or a complete fabrication.

Exercise: Understanding Thoughts and Emotions

To help you with the following exercise, let's look at a hypothetical situation. When answering the questions that follow this story, keep in mind that there is room for variation, because everyone's experience differs.

A. Examine the relationships among thoughts, feelings, and actions. In the story below, see if you can identify the components of the event: the unfiltered emotions, the thought filters used, the filtered emotions, and finally, the actions taken. Your answers may differ somewhat from those provided, which is fine. There's room for various interpretations.

■ *Case Example:* Tom and Lisa's Story

Tom and Lisa had been married for seven years, and the last three were very tumultuous. They had no children but fought daily over money. Tom was a self-proclaimed underearner, just as his father had been. This modesty, which Lisa had initially found attractive, now drove her crazy, especially since Tom was very well educated and had a great deal of artistic talent as a graphic designer. Over the years she became increasingly frustrated, because she felt they could and should have a higher standard of living.

Lisa's income supported them, but she wanted to move into a house with a yard. On the other hand, Tom had lower expectations than his wife had. He felt that they had all they needed in their twelve-hundred-square-foot condo, and as he said, "I don't want to work that hard just to impress a bunch of people I don't even know or care about."

Things really came to a head in their marriage when Tom lost his job. Lisa was so mad, she couldn't speak to Tom for over a week. She thought over and over about the ways he could have improved his work performance, responded better to his boss's evaluation, or even fought to keep his job. She couldn't accept that this had happened and that they now seemed headed for financial ruin. Lisa filed for divorce within a week.

Using this scenario with Lisa and Tom, fill in the following with your best guess:

1. What was the event?

2. What might have been Lisa's unfiltered emotions in response to the event?

3. What meaning might she have given this event?

4. What filtered feelings might she have felt?

5. What action did Lisa take?

6. Do you believe these actions were in response to her unfiltered or filtered emotions, or both? Why do you believe this?

7. Were Lisa's filtered feelings about a past, present, or future scenario? Explain.

Answers: 1. The event was that Tom lost his job. 2. Lisa's unfiltered response was probably fear. 3. The meaning she gave this event was that they were headed for financial ruin and would never achieve her goals. 4. The filtered emotions Lisa added to this event may have been disbelief, blame, disappointment, anger, and more fear. 5. The actions Lisa took were to stop speaking to Tom for a week and then file for divorce. 6. It's not unusual for someone who has lost his or her job to fear financial insecurity, but Lisa certainly took this event and created the worst-case scenario in her mind. Even though they were not necessarily in monetary trouble when Tom was laid off, they weren't where Lisa wanted them to be, so she went into a panic that they would never get there. You can probably see that all of the emotions Lisa experienced sapped her of energy, and since they were almost exclusively driven by her judgments and stories (thought filters), she could have saved a great deal of energy by not entertaining the stories. 7. The feelings were about the past and the future. (Your answers here may be different. As mentioned earlier, filtered emotions vary more, because we each bring our own experiences to the event.)

B. Write in your journal about something in your own life that is bothering you or taking up space in your head, and apply the same set of questions to your personal situation. See if you can distinguish between your unfiltered and filtered emotions.

Energy-Saving Tips

It's normal to have many different thoughts and emotions when considering the fate of your marriage. As mentioned at the beginning of this chapter, by the time most people come to see me, they are extremely drained. They've bounced around, not knowing which end is up or that such emotional turmoil is normal. The amount of time, money, and energy I've seen people expend in this period of their lives is astounding, especially since much of it can be avoided with some basic knowledge.

In an ideal world, you would make every major decision in your life from a tranquil place within yourself. When you are contemplating divorce, it's not always possible to calm *yourself*, let alone other people, places, and things. Also, you don't always have the option to wait until you're calm to make a move. Marital problems stir the waters more than almost any other of life's challenges. That's why distinguishing between your unfiltered and filtered emotions, and monitoring your made-up stories (as well as eventually learning to stop telling yourself stories altogether) can be crucial for maintaining control of your situation.

■ *Case Example:* Mary Beth and Richard's Story

Hindsight is absolutely 20/20. No one knows that better than Mary Beth, a woman who thought she had to make some rash decisions but realized later that rushing into the process cost her much more than if she had waited for her feelings to calm down, created a plan for herself, and sought much more professional guidance.

After reading a book on verbal abuse, Mary Beth was motivated to get away from her controlling and passive-aggressive husband Richard. She felt empowered by the knowledge she had gained, and decided to file right away and serve her husband with papers. She actually felt exhilarated from taking action after suffering for so long.

The problem was that Mary Beth was actually coming from a place of anger and vindictiveness. She wanted to pay Richard back for all the pain he had caused her, so she had him served at work, causing him severe public humiliation, and then proceeded to hire a very nasty attorney, who stirred up controversy right away.

Before she realized it, Mary Beth was embroiled in an incredibly contentious marital dissolution process. On receiving her first legal bill, she nearly fell over. She had had no idea how quickly the billable hours added up. To make matters more confusing for her, she started having feelings of remorse and began questioning whether she should leave after all.

Mary Beth had moved too quickly and had not obtained sufficient emotional, legal, or financial advice or support. She was on a runaway train and soon found herself in deep remorse. Luckily for her, she realized in time that she could step back and really contemplate how to proceed. Despite her attorney's urgings to move forward, Mary Beth listened to her internal guidance system, fired her attorney, and got off the adversarial track.

Richard, who was quite devastated by Mary Beth's actions, voluntarily signed up for a two-year anger management program. He realized that he had mistreated Mary Beth and the kids, and wanted to save his family.

One could argue that if Mary Beth had not taken such drastic actions, Richard would not have gotten the message that she would no longer tolerate his abuse, but perhaps they could have saved some time, money, and energy by taking a different tack.

The following tips will help you use your resources wisely. These tips include giving yourself enough time to sort out all of your emotions (distinguish unfiltered from filtered), get clear about your goals and separate your goals from your emotions, gather as much information about your situation as possible, get professional feedback and support, and make a plan of action.

Take the Time You Need

With very few exceptions, there are no emergencies or reasons to rush your decision-making process. The exceptions include if you or your children are in danger of being abused by your spouse, or you are in danger of abusing your children or your spouse. If either of these situations applies to you, I can't recommend enough that you get professional help from therapists, doctors, and attorneys as soon as possible. You will benefit tremendously from professional guidance.

If you do not fall into one of those two categories, then you would do well to take your time and not let anyone push you into making decisions, including your spouse or your attorney. Trust yourself and check in often with yourself about whether you feel pressured or antsy about your situation. There won't always be an indicator that your timing is right, but there are definitely internal alarms that go off when you are not going at your own pace.

Gathering more support and information will probably help you feel better, get you what you need faster, and spare you from having to backtrack later on.

Distinguish Filtered from Unfiltered Emotions

I've seen many people try to move too quickly through the decision-making process as a way of avoiding their unfiltered feelings of sadness or anger at not getting their needs and desires met, or the vulnerability of having to ask for what they needed. In any case, when people avoid or become out of touch with their true emotions but continue forging ahead, all roads lead to regret. This is true, whether they stay married or divorce.

When husbands or wives dismiss their real feelings and force themselves to stay in an unhealthy situation, they are almost always filled with resentment, anger, and depression from the belief that they are trapped.

And usually when people are trying to get through divorce too quickly, as Mary Beth was, they are driven purely by their filtered emotions, which are propelled by whatever story they made up. They are usually making decisions based on anger over the past or fear of the future. Even though unfiltered feelings arise initially, they are pushed underground and ignored all too often as the thought filters and resulting filtered emotions take over.

Separate Your Goals from Your Emotions

If you look back at Ron and Cheryl's story, you will remember that Ron wanted a divorce because he didn't like how he felt around Cheryl. She made him feel small and worthless, just as his father had done.

The goal in this case was not so much for Ron to get away from Cheryl as it was for him to feel better about himself. If Ron had not sought counseling, he might have let his goals be colored by his emotions. Instead, he was able to get clearer with what he was really looking for.

Just as people stay married for the wrong reasons, many people divorce for the wrong reasons. By implementing these tips, you will much more likely take the right action for the right reasons.

Gather the Information You Need

By reading this book, you are gathering some important information about the emotional aspects of marriage, separation, and divorce. There are many more books out there on the subject (refer to the suggested reading list in the back of the book), as well as endless articles, websites, and other Internet resources.

You can consult with an attorney, just to get an understanding of your rights in the event of divorce. This can get expensive but could be well worth the money you invest.

Talk to friends, family, neighbors, and coworkers who have either been through divorce or had near misses and stayed married. The more personal accounts you hear on the subject, the better perspective you can have on your own marital situation. However, if you find yourself feeling more confused than clear, limit your discussions to people with whom you share the most similarities.

Get Feedback and Support

Not only do you not have to take this journey alone, you shouldn't. Get honest, objective feedback and support about whether you're headed in the right direction, what steps you need to take next, and what resources you will need. If friends and family can provide this, that's fine, but a trained professional who specializes in divorce will be of utmost help to you. There are often local, low-cost legal and mental health resources available.

Make a Plan

Once you have consulted with a professional specializing in marital issues or divorce (or both), you will have the foundation of information you need to create a structured plan for how to proceed. Have several plans if necessary, but lay out some viable options for yourself (and your children) so you can take care of yourself. Doing nothing and waiting for things to change is the best way to delude yourself into more pain. Your plans may need ongoing revisions as your situation changes, but knowing what you need and doing what you can to meet those needs will help you immensely.

A plan should start with identifying your ideal goal and then the steps you'll need to take to reach it. Here is an example:

Plan A: My ideal goal is for my spouse and me to reconcile our marriage. Steps to get there: (1) contact him and let him know that I'd like us to talk, (2) find a neutral meeting place and set a time to meet, (3) write out what I'd like to say (for example, what I need from him to allow him back into the house and the consequences if he can't honor these requests), (4) run this by my therapist and my friend Kristin for feedback. Plan B: If we can't reconcile, I want to get a divorce. Steps to get there: (1) file papers with the court, (2) decide which divorce format to use (mediation, collaborative, or litigation), (3) find an attorney (ask friends and my neighbor Stefan), (4) tell the kids.

Your plans may include as many or as few details as you need to write. They can outline whom to confide in when things get difficult for you and your spouse, having an alternative place to stay, hunting for your own house or apartment, knowing your legal rights, understanding your financial situation, going back to school, establishing credit in your own name, and much more.

Generally, anything that empowers you in your current marital flux and helps you identify your choices constitutes a plan. If you can't get this going on your own, it's fine to ask for assistance from others in putting pen to paper. If you get an answer from one resource that doesn't sit well, it's wise to ask for another opinion. Don't cut corners if you can help it. Because making a plan is such a beneficial tool in gaining clarity, I strongly recommend not putting it off.

Exercise: Doing What You Can

People sometimes leave their marriages too quickly because they are in pain or just want life to be easier. It is only later when they feel remorseful and realize they could have and should have done more to keep the marriage together.

The following questions will help you examine what actions you have taken thus far to keep your marriage together and to work on improving your relationship with your spouse.

1. Do you feel pressured to make a decision, or are you ignoring the issues in hopes they will go away? Describe your feelings as you decide what to do next (for instance, stress and anxiety, numbness, or a dull ache). Extreme emotions may indicate that you are succumbing to external pressure or to your own denial.

2. List possible ways or reasons you believe you may be taking too long and avoiding coming to a decision about your marriage. Then list possible ways in which you might be letting outside forces pressure you into making a hasty decision.

3. How are you dealing with your emotions? Are you making decisions from an emotionally calm (you sense an inner calm and grounded-

ness) or tumultuous place (your stomach is in knots all the time, and you feel quite moody) within yourself?

4. Are you clear about your long- and short-term goals? If not, what do you need to get clarity?

5. What facts and information have you gathered about saving your marriage, separating, or divorcing? What additional information do you need to obtain?

6. How are you getting support and feedback for your marital situation? In what ways do you need to get more support or feedback?

7. What plans do you have in place for taking care of yourself, your marriage, and your children? What have you already done? What more do you need to do?

I recommend answering these questions on your own first and then with a trusted friend, therapist, clergy, or confidant. Because we all have blind spots, there may be important pieces of this process that you cannot see on your own.

Sticking with the Process

In closing this chapter, I want to acknowledge the hard work you have done and are doing for yourself by reading this book. By formally examining your thoughts and feelings about your marriage, you have just come through some of the most challenging aspects of your decision-making process.

It may feel daunting to proceed with the rest of the book, and you can certainly take a break if you need to. Contemplating divorce is a sometimes excruciating process. If this were easy, you would be through it by now. Stay with this material and you will learn a great deal more about yourself and your marriage.

4

Learning About Your Relationship

When two people are under the influence of the most violent, most insane, most delusive, and most transient of passions, they are required to swear that they will remain in that excited, abnormal, and exhausting condition until death do them part.

—George Bernard Shaw

I have found that once a couple understands the mechanics behind their relationship—specifically, why they were attracted to each other in the beginning and why they now have marital problems—they can often do more to improve their situation. You can't change what you're not conscious of, so a big part of working on yourself and your relationship is "looking under the hood" to see the inner workings of how this machine you call your "marriage" operates.

But before moving into understanding the dynamics of your marital relationship, let's review what you have learned so far:

In chapter 1, you identified the mental process you have experienced while contemplating divorce; in chapter 2, you learned about what options are available to you with regard to your marriage; in chapter 3, you acknowledged the many feelings you have had (and will have) in your decision-making process, and learned tools for understanding and even controlling the emotional ups and downs. You probably have a better perspective on yourself and your situation, as well as your desires and needs, after reading the first three chapters.

This chapter will highlight for you how your thoughts and emotions came into play during the initial attraction you and your spouse shared, as well as how this magnetic force impacts your decision to stay or go. You'll also have a better understanding of how the aspects of your spouse that attracted you initially may be the same ones that are now hurting your relationship.

How and Why We Attract Someone

Why do we attract a particular mate, and what is it about him or her that attracts us? How do we go from this initial attraction to falling in love and, shortly thereafter, settling into unconscious behavior patterns? What is at work to set these dynamics into play? And how do we miss seeing the patterns more clearly? Can we have more control over changing the interactions we dislike?

Physical attraction and sexual allure can act as powerful magnets that initially bring two people together. People often marry based primarily on sexual attraction, but unless there is a more meaningful connection, the marriage won't likely be fulfilling.

In deeper long-term relationships, there are three main reasons we come together and stay with our chosen mates: (1) to feel comfort, (2) to find balance, and (3) to heal old wounds.

Seeking Comfort

Humans have long been referred to as "creatures of comfort" because of our tendency to seek out people, places, and things that feel familiar. This is true even when the something or someone is not good or healthy for us. I call this *unconscious gravitation*, because we are pulled toward the other person by the subtleties of what we are accustomed to.

Case Example: Donald and Myra's Story

It was no surprise to me why this young couple was attracted to each other and hooked together like two puzzle pieces. Donald was from an upper-middle-class background with a very strict mother, and Myra was from a more laid-back, commune-style upbringing. At first glance, it seemed an odd match, but it became clear relatively quickly what the core dynamic was that brought them together.

Donald was a self-proclaimed rebel. Everything his family stood for repulsed him, and he wanted to experience as much of an alternative lifestyle as possible. If it hadn't been for Myra's pushing to get married, he would not have conformed to this "oppressive social structure." He hated living "in the box," and freedom was important to him.

Once married, Donald suggested that they have an open marriage. Interestingly enough, this was what Myra grew up with: her parents had agreed to the option of having other relationships outside of their marriage. But soon after consenting to this free-for-all arrangement, Myra's mother had decided that she didn't want to have other intimate relationships (thus, no more open marriage) and became upset with her husband for continuing to see other women.

It set up a dynamic wherein Myra witnessed her mother suffer an incredible amount of pain because of her father's unwillingness to commit to the marriage. Myra had also been hurt by the sense of abandonment she felt over her father's hardly ever being home.

Myra was vehemently opposed to Donald's seeing other women, and let him know that this was unacceptable. Donald saw this as a challenge and an opportunity to repeat his rebellious ways.

Myra repeated an old familiar pattern of her own that she had seen played out with her parents. It was now her husband (not her father) who was unfaithful. It brought up tremendous unhealed pain for her, that of being abandoned and feeling unloved, yet she was used to equating marriage with pain and struggle, so this was nothing out of the ordinary to her.

On the other hand, Donald re-created the dynamic he had grown up with, in the sense that his mother had been on his father's case (and his) for every little thing. He took on the role of acting out and playing the bad guy in his marriage as he had done in his family of origin.

Donald was a comfortable fit with Myra, because he was absent more often than not and because he took on the role of the bad boy. Myra fit comfortably with Donald because she was angry at him all the time; she was like his chastising mother.

It didn't occur to either that they had the choice to stay together and change, or leave. They both just assumed that this duress was the norm in relationships, so they lived with it for a very long time.

When the dynamic is unfamiliar, the couple usually won't get together or stay together. I once saw a man in my practice who lamented that over the years he'd met dozens of powerful, attractive, very "with it" women yet kept getting into relationships with women who were extremely needy and dependent, exactly as his mother had been. He wanted to find a woman he knew was healthy, but the attraction just wasn't there. Instead, he kept gravitating toward the familiar, despite the fact that he consciously wanted a more equal partner.

Another male client mentioned having gone out with a beautiful woman, but when, on the third date, he saw what a temper she had, the attraction was over. His family had been relatively mild mannered, and he didn't want to be treated badly by anyone. He assumed that if she showed this level of ire toward him on the third date, what would she be like once the mask came off? Because this trait was unfamiliar, it was noticeably divergent from what he sought in a partner.

In both of these examples, these men were not attracted to qualities in the women that were unfamiliar to them. Regardless of whether a trait is healthy or unhealthy, when it is familiar, it has a powerful magnetism. More often than not, the people involved don't even know that it could be different, so they stick with what they know, even when they are hurt by it somehow.

I have one more example of the pull that the familiar can have on us. A woman who joined one of my groups did nothing but complain session after session about all the rotten things her husband had said or done to her, despite her attempts to get him to stop. When I asked her what her part in the dynamic was, she had absolutely no idea. The answer was simple: she stayed with him.

She had tried to intervene by getting him into couples counseling and telling him not to speak or act disrespectfully toward her, but he disregarded her requests. It never occurred to her to leave, not because she felt divorce wasn't an option, but because this relationship dynamic was familiar to her. She didn't know that spouses could relate differently to each other.

Exercise: Staying in Your Comfort Zone

We all need some comfort to feel safe and to grow. However, seeking comfort (especially too much comfort) can have its downsides. For instance, by staying too comfortable, you might not grow emotionally or might repeat unconscious patterns that don't serve you very well. This exercise will help you uncover ways in which you perhaps unknowingly gravitated to the comfort of your spouse and how, together, you may have slipped into comfortable ways of relating.

1. What level of comfort did you feel with your spouse early in your relationship with him or her? Describe the traits or behaviors your spouse demonstrated that made you feel at ease.

2. Do you remember what particular trait or behavior made you feel this sense of comfort or knowing with your spouse?

3. Can you name three to five qualities in your spouse that are also in one of your parents or siblings?

4. Which of these qualities, if any, has a strong emotional charge for you (you either love or strongly dislike this quality)?

5. Can you identify any familiar patterns that you and your spouse have slipped into (patterns you saw in your parents)?

Write in your journal about any awareness you gained from this exercise. Then write about how gravitating to the familiar may have kept you engaged in some unhealthy dynamics with your spouse. If you can see how this has impacted other areas of your life as well, such as work and with friends, write about that too.

Balancing Acts

The second force at work in bringing couples together is the need to find balance. The law of attraction states: "That which is likened unto itself is drawn unto itself" (Hicks and Hicks 2004, 50). We've also heard the sayings "Water seeks its own level" and "Like attracts like."

Yet, we have also heard the expression "Opposites attract," and have surely witnessed this phenomenon when noticing, for example, an introvert latch onto an extrovert, a very rational type hook up with a highly emotional person, or a slob and a neat freak fall in love.

The reason why opposites attract is the same reason why like attracts like: every living organism in nature seeks homeostasis or stability to remain alive and function well. Humans, and human relationships, are no exception.

A relatively balanced person will be attracted to another relatively balanced person. He or she won't usually relate to an unstable person. On the contrary, individuals who are out of equilibrium within themselves will be most attracted to partners who they believe can complete or balance them.

While I have never seen a relationship that didn't involve an ongoing dance of some sort to find or maintain balance, a relationship wherein one person *needs* the other to complete him or her usually has a much more tumultuous dynamic. In addition, the impact of one partner's leaving is often greater when there is a component of instability to begin with. The following diagram illustrates this point:

FIGURE 5: DIAGRAM OF INTERRELATIONAL BALANCE

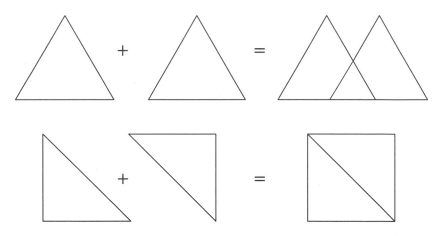

In the first set of triangles, two balanced people are represented by two equilateral triangles side by side. When the balanced couple interacts, they create a third, smaller triangle, which represents their interdependence. They don't need each other to be balanced and can therefore function well as individual units or as an interdependent unit.

In the second set of triangles, a hypotenuse triangle next to an inverted hypotenuse triangle represents two people who come together to complete each other. When these two hypotenuse triangles join, they make up a balanced unit, a square, and can only maintain this balance together; they cannot stand alone and be balanced as the equilateral triangles can.

What does it mean to be in or out of balance? While we may not be aware of it, we actually possess every quality of what it is to be human. We can be sweet and mean; impatient and patient; silly and serious; neat and sloppy. Our unique personalities are partly based on the temperaments we were born with and partly derived from learning what helped us get our survival needs met as young children.

One child in the family may learn that he gets his needs met by being responsible and taking care of his younger siblings; another discovers that the louder and more aggressive she is, the more her parents pay attention to her and give her what she wants; and still another child may find that being the entertainment committee may win over the love and approval of others.

Other factors involved in determining which of our traits emerge and which remain dormant (or in the background) include dynamics such as the number of siblings and the parenting abilities of the mother and father, as well as what they model for behavior; birth order; cultural, familial, and religious norms; and tension levels in the home. This is a complicated process, but the end result is that we each have varying levels of all human traits, the combination of which distinguishes one individual from another—and you from your spouse.

A balanced individual can give and receive, be extroverted sometimes and introverted other times, express a full range of emotions (in a balanced way), admit when he or she's wrong, and accept praise for a job well done. Being balanced does not necessarily mean that we *demonstrate* equal amounts of all traits, but it does require that we *acknowledge* these traits equally and fully *accept* our humanness.

If there was ever a time in your life when you tried to overcompensate for your anger by being extra nice to others—when, pretending you had no needs, you gave to others and never asked for anything in return, or when you ignored your grief and tried to forge ahead with a smile on your face—then you know what it feels like to be off balance.

■ *Case Example:* Claire's Story

Early one December, when Claire first came to see me, she told me that she wouldn't even think about divorcing until after Christmas. She went on to explain how special this time of year was to her and her children. Every Christmas, she went all out, decorating the house, the yard, and even the cars. She and her kids put up twenty Santas, hung Christmas lights everywhere, displayed wreaths on every door, bought a huge tree, and spent hours decorating it. Claire added that she always bought tons of presents for the kids and felt that she could never overdo this holiday.

I encouraged her to tell me more about why it needed to be so spectacular. She admitted that she had done this to avoid the painful memory of her father's walking out on Christmas Eve when she was eight years old. She never saw her father again, which was a tremendous loss for her. Claire didn't want her children to associate Christmas with anything except utter joy and abundance, so she always exaggerated the positive aspects of the season.

When she came in for a session one day later that month, she knew that this would be her last Christmas with her husband. Years of grief caught up with her. Revisiting her past was tougher than she had thought it would be, but she was ready. By feeling and accepting the emotions surrounding her loss, Claire came more into her center and no longer had to drive herself into the ground during the holidays. It didn't have to be so fabulous to distract from what had been so devastating. A few months later she reported that she felt as if she had lost 150 pounds and had a renewed sense of energy.

Exercise: Where Are You Out of Balance?

By answering the following questions, you can begin to understand some of the dynamics within your personality. This is by no means a comprehensive list, so feel free to add your own qualities here.

A. Assess where you personally may be out of balance in the following areas, as well as in any other areas that stand out for you:

   1. Are you highly emotional or unemotional?

   2. Are you an overly dependent or independent person?

   3. Are you a spendthrift or a penny-pincher?

   4. Are you very driven or very relaxed?

   5. Are you a control freak or very laid back?

   6. Do you seek out challenges or avoid them at all costs?

   7. Are you highly sexual or asexual?

8. Are you very silly or serious?

9. Are you selective about the company you keep, or open and loving to everyone?

10. Are you politically liberal or conservative?

B. List any other qualities that come to mind that cause extreme emotions or make you feel out of balance: _____

_____

C. If you can, write down others' beliefs, events, or behaviors that you believe may have shaped your behavior and caused you to lean heavily toward one extreme of a personality trait. For example, someone who was poor growing up may feel a stronger need to save money than someone for whom money wasn't so lacking.

D. If you have realized that you operate from an extreme place to balance out or counteract one of your spouse's traits, describe what steps you can take to come more into balance with *yourself* and become less reactionary in relation to him or her. For example, you realize that you are extremely suspicious of everyone and everything because your spouse is so naive. Can you practice trust even when your spouse continues to be overly trusting?

<hr>

You now have an idea of how balance that is based on compensating for your partner's traits can operate in you, and you can apply these principles to your marriage. When two people come together, they form one unit. This new unit, which is a combination of your beliefs and traits, and those of your spouse, will form an entirely new personality.

Your spouse will unconsciously trigger certain traits in you to emerge in greater or lesser intensity, depending on what makes your marital system more balanced. Likewise, your traits complement or contradict different traits in your spouse.

Let's look at the example of someone who grew up with little money. As an adult, he saves every extra penny he can for a rainy day, because having a cushion in the bank makes him feel more secure. If he marries a woman who doesn't share this value and likes to spend the family money, his security will be threatened, throwing off the balance in their marital system. He will feel inclined to save more, because she spends more. On the other hand, if he marries someone who also likes adding to the savings account every month, his inner miser won't have to work so hard.

When you and your spouse possess opposing qualities, it creates a dynamic I call *unconscious polarization*. Using the above example, you can see that, to maintain balance between the two opposite qualities, the miser feels more of a need to hoard money in response to the overspender's spending. The more the miser hoards, the more the spendthrift feels she can spend, which makes the miser hoard more. As the tension increases over how to handle finances, each spouse's behavior gets more extreme. Before the couple realizes it, they are both positioned firmly in their opposing corners with a well-developed habit of butting heads.

Exercise: Where Is Your Relationship Out of Balance?

Eight main relationship areas are listed below, along with extra space for you to add your own areas. Referring to these topics, answer the questions below and see what you notice about the balance (or imbalance) of each in your marriage:

Financially	Sexually
Parentally	Emotionally
Physically	Mentally
Spiritually	Politically

_____   _____

1. How are you and your spouse alike in each area listed above?

2. How are you different in these areas?

3. How do you balance each other out? Do you notice ways in which you leave your own comfort zone or norm to balance your spouse?

4. How do you feel about that?

5. What other observations do you want to note about the dynamics/ balance between you and your spouse?

If you are like most people, you may have known some of the ways you and your spouse differ but may not have consciously been aware that you came together to find balance. Not only was the attraction to each other neither mistake nor coincidence, it was born from a very healthy and natural desire to find homeostasis. It is only when both spouses get caught in the dynamic of unconscious polarization that this dance to find balance can become destructive.

Healing Old Wounds

The third and final force that intimately connects two people is the need to heal old wounds. I can't tell you how many times a client has said to me, "If only my wife would stop being abusive, we could stay together" or "If only my husband wouldn't carouse so much, we could have a good relationship."

What these people don't understand is that the situations they have with their spouses can actually help them uncover wounds they might not even know are there. It's not necessarily what happens that matters, but it's how we react to what happens that indicates how we feel about ourselves and what value we place on ourselves. People who stay in situations such as those mentioned above believe that they deserve the treatment they receive. If they didn't, they would leave.

This concept is sometimes difficult for people to grasp. A case in point entails a woman I explained this to in a session one evening. She became indignant when I mentioned our attracting people and situations to us so that we could heal. She shouted, "You mean to tell me that I *attracted* a cheating husband and that it's *my* fault he slept with all my friends?" I assured her that I did not mean to imply that it was her fault, but I did point out to her that she had *stayed* with him despite his having cheated on her many times. She had a belief (that likely originated well before she met him, in early childhood) that she deserved to be treated badly or that she wasn't enough.

She couldn't deny that each time her husband had cheated on her it reinforced the old unworthy tapes she had played in her head her entire life. This woman understood that, had she known in her heart that she didn't deserve to be betrayed, she would have kicked him out after the first incident or, at the very least, would not have simply looked the other way.

We are creatures of habit and, as such, stick to what is familiar in others or the familiar ways others make us feel. Often, the dynamic you slip into with your partner is similar to, or ironically completely the opposite of, a dynamic that existed in your family of origin. You unknowingly learned an unhealthy way of relating to your family, which you now bring into your relationships with your spouse and your children.

This is true even if you developed a way of being that is diametrically opposed to the behavior of the family member you didn't want to be like. It's as if you have blind spots through which these familiar and comfortable people and patterns slide past your awareness.

I call this *unconscious navigation*. More times than not, this unhealthy interaction resembles, or is in reaction to, a dynamic you had with one of your parents, the one with whom you have the most unresolved issues. This is not necessarily a bad thing unless you keep finding yourself in relationship patterns that cause you pain or anguish. Such patterns don't normally come to your attention until they become painful, so it is usually the dysfunctional dynamics that get in the way of your relationships.

■ Case Example: Jessica's Story

Jessica came to me just as her marriage was ending. She was devastated and angry all at once after her husband's disclosure that he wanted to get a divorce. As she saw it, she had been "the perfect wife," because she was agreeable, easygoing, and fun to be with. An example she offered to illustrate her generosity was when her husband, Dave, wanted her to stop working and stay home with the kids. Despite her inner urging to maintain a career, she had agreed to quit her job and become a full-time mom. She didn't question his judgment or acknowledge her wants and needs. Although she felt that her children had benefited greatly, she realized that she had given up her power by making this move.

When we further explored the dynamics in the relationship, Jessica told me that she had rarely stood up for herself when she should have. Dave had always gotten his way, and still, he left. When I suggested that perhaps he left because he got his way all the time, she clearly had no idea what I meant.

Before explaining, I asked her to tell me about her parents' relationship. She said that both her parents were from traditional backgrounds, and she was raised to believe that the man "wore the pants" in the family. I prompted her to elaborate on this, and she revealed that her mother had never been allowed to give input when it came to major decisions for the family. She remembered a time when her father had gotten a new job that required the family to relocate out of state. Her mother, who was pregnant with Jessica's younger brother at the time, had expressed that she did not want to go because she didn't want to have to find all new doctors, hospitals, schools, and child care.

This was the one and only time Jessica ever heard her mother stand up for herself, and boy, did she pay for it. Jessica said that the yelling that ensued scared her half to death. She remembered sitting by her bedroom door, ready to go to her mother's aid if need be. Her father was so angry that her mother dared try to interfere that he said he wasn't asking for her opinion, he was telling her that they were moving. That comment made Jessica vow that she would never marry a man who treated her like that. She felt disappointed that her mother didn't have more of a backbone.

I had her describe more about what had first attracted her to Dave and why she felt they had come together. She said that he had been her boss at a job she'd had when she was younger, and she had always liked his style. He had been fair and tended to bring out the best in people. She said that he had seemed to know what he wanted, which made her feel secure. Right away, I helped her realize that he was more or less an authority figure to her and that perhaps she liked his being in charge. Jessica had never thought of it that way but agreed that she probably felt unconsciously attracted to his domineering presence.

She could also look back and admit that, even though Dave was much more open minded and fair than her own father had been, she had always been afraid to question him for fear he would yell at her, just as her father had done to her mother, or worse, that he would leave her. Jessica saw that she had compromised her own desires thousands of times as a result of this fear, and the lightbulb went on for her about what Dave had meant when he had stated that he had lost respect for her. Now it made sense.

People don't respect those who fail to take a stand for themselves and allow others to push them around. Jessica realized that she had played a major role in setting things up, by assuming she would get in trouble if she expressed her needs and wants to Dave. Though designed to preserve the marriage, her compliant strategy had backfired. Dave wanted more from a partner.

It's not always so easy to identify the unhealed wound, but in this case it was fairly obvious. Jessica had seen her mother treated as a slave by her misogynistic father. With four small children, her mother was too afraid to go out on her own, so instead she stayed and allowed a part of her spirit to be broken. Jessica did not marry her father, but she did mimic the actions of her mother in becoming a people pleaser and playing a subservient role, thus opening the way for Dave to simultaneously take advantage of and lose respect for her.

Jessica's unhealed wound was from her internalized abusive father, who had always gotten on her case before she even opened her mouth. This mental chatter would tell her not to stir the waters, not to make things difficult, and on and on. She perpetuated the unspoken beliefs that women's needs were less important than men's, she needed her husband in order to survive, and as long as appearances were maintained, she was doing well in her marriage.

Clearly, the learning for Jessica was to stop pleasing others and putting their needs first, and to start taking a stand for herself.

■ *Case Example:* Pat's Story

Pat was fired suddenly and unjustly, and then dumped by a friend in the same way. Both of these events occurred within a six-month period. I asked him to tell me what beliefs came up for him, and he answered that he felt as if he had nothing to offer. When I inquired when he had ever felt this before, he responded that he had often felt that way around his father, who had treated him disdainfully and been extremely impatient when Pat couldn't quickly learn whatever it was his father was trying to teach him.

Pat had been through two failed marriages, which he could rationalize, but losing his job and his best friend in such a short span truly devastated him. He believed that the universe was punishing him for not having been a good husband. When I asked him to explain why he hadn't been what he considered a good husband, he said that he didn't have a clue what being a husband meant! He had assumed that each wife would leave him sooner or later, so he hadn't put much effort into either relationship. In both cases, the women he'd married told him he was a no-good louse.

His lack of confidence and knowledge about what being a husband called for had caused him to shrink and participate little in either marriage. His lack of participation is what had caused his wives to get fed up and dump him.

Once Pat understood this dynamic, he had an epiphany about what went wrong at work and with his friend: just as in his marriages, the reason he was laid off and dumped by his best friend was because he had not fully participated and given his all. He had shown up at work, done the absolute minimum required of him, and collected his paycheck.

He had never volunteered to stay late or take on extra jobs, and hadn't cared that he had never been promoted.

Although never able to talk to his friend about what had transpired between them, he surmised that, there too, he had gone a bit too far in requesting favors of his friend while being unavailable when his friend had asked him to reciprocate. Pat said that every time his friend had asked him to do something, he had gone into a panic because he didn't have the same skill set as his friend and assumed he would disappoint him.

Pat saw that his low sense of self-worth created self-fulfilling prophecies that caused everyone and everything he cared about to leave. Through his immense pain, he saw that he had some serious work to do in building self-confidence and even self-love.

Exercise: Healing Your Wounds

The following exercise asks you to look within to uncover what old wounds you might have that still need healing. If you can't come up with answers, ask a sibling, a friend, or perhaps a therapist for assistance. Those close to you or a professional dealing with such issues may have insights into you and your life in areas where you have a blind spot. Write the answers to these questions in your journal:

1. In looking at your own relationship history, identify patterns of dynamics you have experienced repeatedly (for instance, always attracting someone with anger management problems or attracting especially dependent and needy partners).

2. Why do you believe you keep drawing this dynamic into your life?

3. What emotional or mental wounds do you have that you believe need healing?

4. Describe how those wounds have affected other relationships or situations in your life.

Because the information you just got in touch with is sensitive, you may want to seek professional support from a therapist to help you process what you learned, and find more clarity about what your wounds are and how you can heal them.

The first step in healing your wounds is in knowing that they are there and what they are made of. In this next section, we will explore ways to heal these old wounds.

Breaking Patterns

Maladaptive patterns in relationships never occur in a vacuum. This is not to say that one or the other spouse is necessarily to blame for the problems a couple encounters, but both interact *with one another* to create relationship dynamics. One acts, and the other reacts. The first then reacts to the other's reaction, prompting another reaction, and so on in an endless cycle.

Because any relationship is made up of interdependent patterns created by both partners together, once you understand how and why certain unhealthy relationship patterns are established, you can begin to change the dynamic.

The good news is that it often only takes one partner to change for the entire marital system to change. What this means to you is that, with some awareness and work, you may be able to redirect the course of your marriage or your life by altering how you act or react. When you behave differently, those around you react to you differently.

However, I will reiterate that you can't force others to change and that this should not be your motive for changing your behavior. You are altering your behavior to become more balanced within yourself. If your spouse is able to match you on this healthier level, the marriage will likely survive. If he or she can't or won't rise to your new level of interaction, the odds of having a healthy relationship with that person are slim to none.

Certainly, there are some people who are more set in their patterns than others. For example, some may be unwilling or incapable of refraining from violence, have addictions or past hurts that will never heal, or have untreatable mental illnesses. And there are some with less grave issues who simply don't want to change, so they don't, and nothing you do—even threatening to leave—will motivate them to change.

I want to reiterate that I don't endorse using the threat of divorce as a weapon or manipulation. Just note that, after you tell your spouse you want out, if he or she doesn't snap to at the potential of losing you, pay attention. This may indicate that your partner has no intention of ever changing.

I have seen many people (usually women, because we are often raised to acquiesce to the needs of others) do *all* the work to maintain a relationship, thinking that if they just try harder or do more, they will be able to change an unhealthy pattern. The one putting in the effort and energy toward preserving the relationship is usually perpetually exhausted and eventually becomes quite angry, while the unaware spouse goes about life disregarding all the hard work his or her partner is doing to try to keep things afloat. This is definitely not a healthy or balanced pattern to get into and will more than likely lead to a mental, emotional, or nuptial meltdown.

After changing what you can, if you notice little or no results, you may have to seriously rethink whether the relationship is worth maintaining or if you are struggling to keep a sinking ship afloat.

In a perfect world, both partners are motivated to improve the relationship together, and each has the ability to accept responsibility for his or her part in the marital discord. As previously mentioned, it is almost never just one person's fault or responsibility when a couple arrives at an impasse in the relationship. How often have we heard "It takes two to tango"?

You may feel very strongly that your spouse's behavior is the problem in your relationship and that you are perfectly justified in your actions and reactions. But until you understand that you play a part in maintaining unhealthy patterns by accepting the unacceptable, not drawing boundaries, not speaking your mind, failing to ask for what you need, or biting the bait your spouse sets out for you, you will perpetuate the pattern.

This chapter has shown some examples of how this phenomenon plays out. The following stories are about three couples who were able to change themselves, and therefore attract a new type of partner, as in the first story, or turn a negative and destructive pattern around, as in the second and third stories.

The last two accounts are particularly important for you to see how couples can reverse patterns after interacting for many years in a dynamic that didn't work well. Using some of this awareness to turn around a pattern or dynamic in your marriage may determine the outcome of your situation.

■ *Case Example:* Paul and Yvonne's Story

At age twenty-five Yvonne came to see me to explore a pattern she had identified in herself of having a string of unavailable and sometimes abusive boyfriends. During one of our initial sessions, I asked Yvonne to tell me about her upbringing. She reported that both of her parents were alcoholics who argued all the time. Yvonne avoided alcohol and, because she had seen the problems anger caused in relationships, had decided not to let herself get that mad. At the very least, she was determined not to show it if she got upset.

Vowing never to repeat the abuses she had witnessed, Yvonne worked hard on herself. Before she came to see me, she had been to 12-step programs, read many self-help books, developed a spiritual practice, and gone on antidepressants. Because she viewed anger as a "bad emotion," her previous recovery work had been about trying to make it go away.

I was able to help Yvonne see that she had not allowed herself to experience the whole range of human emotions, which had prevented her from being fully available in a relationship. It made sense that she had continued attracting men who were angry and unavailable. These men provided the balance against her overly abundant kindness and represented parts of herself that she needed to reclaim.

Since we can't get rid of any aspect of ourselves, whenever there is a trait or emotion that we possess but try to deny, it continually shows up in the world around us. As I mentioned in chapter 3, our emotions are like little kids who are trying to get our attention. Instead of going away when ignored, they scream louder. They must be heard!

Through some intense anger management work we did together for over two years, Yvonne was able to see just how and when she pushed her anger away. In time, she learned that her feelings would not kill her (as she had feared) and became willing to feel angry, sad, and even enraged at times.

At age thirty-two, Yvonne returned to therapy with me after meeting Paul, a man she would later marry. The two had met in a class at a local community college. In class Paul was the quiet, studious type who only spoke when called on, while Yvonne asked lots of questions and was often quite outspoken.

They never would have gotten to know each other had it not been for a class project they were assigned to complete together. Both realized how much they liked each other and how good each felt being around the other. Yvonne said that she was sure that if she had not done as much inner work, she would not have looked twice at such a great guy as Paul.

According to Yvonne, Paul came from a pretty healthy family. Other than, as a kid, wishing that they had had more money, he couldn't remember his family having any major problems. His parents didn't fight much, and loved him and his brothers deeply. They had been terrific role models.

Yvonne said that Paul would be the first to admit that his family had had their issues, but his parents had been there for him whenever he needed them and were supportive of his being who he was. They didn't try to mold him into someone he was not.

Yvonne asked Paul what his parents had modeled for him about fighting, and he responded that, while they had had occasional disputes, they had never raised their voices or become abusive and always worked through the disagreement in the moment. He also told Yvonne that there was plenty of love and affection between his parents, even when they represented opposite sides of an issue.

In her eventual marriage, Yvonne found that she and Paul could argue without having their worlds crumble. She could say what she needed to without his flying off the handle, and vice versa. Paul never threatened to leave Yvonne or punish her when she expressed herself. He allowed her to be the whole person that she was.

Yvonne went from the belief that a good relationship involved no fighting to one in which both parties could express an entire range of emotions without anyone hurting, abandoning, lashing out, or manipulating the other.

This is a wonderful example not only of two relatively balanced people coming together but also of someone from an unstable family background (that had rendered her imbalanced) coming into equilibrium with herself so that she could match up with a healthy partner. Through some deep inner work, Yvonne was able to overcome her family's imbalance and find her true, centered self. In turn, she found a solid man to form a new, healthy family with and broke the cycle of dysfunction in her own family.

■ *Case Example:* Kirk and Mindy's Story

Married for fourteen years and having dated for ten years before that, Kirk and Mindy knew each other pretty well. They had basically grown up together, meeting as teenagers in a military housing development where both of their fathers were stationed.

Like so many couples, they had relatively few arguments until they had children. Almost from the time the first diaper was changed, it was apparent that their parenting styles were polar opposites. Both Kirk and Mindy had strict parents, which caused Kirk to become a strict father, while Mindy vowed to be a different type of parent, one who was much more flexible.

In Kirk's eyes, Mindy was too wishy-washy and lenient, whereas to Mindy, Kirk was too rigid and unreasonable. Kirk believed that parents should let their children cry and feed them only when it was time to eat, while Mindy felt that no child should be left to cry endlessly and worried how such suffering would impact her newborn infant. Kirk and Mindy continued disagreeing from then on.

After two children and thousands of fights later, this couple found themselves in my office discussing divorce. Both were tired of trying to convince the other that their way was the best way. Both recognized that the kids had learned how to play one parent against the other to get what they wanted and that their lack of a united front was hurting everyone, in particular, their marriage.

The trick was getting them to move toward the middle from their respective extremes. Rather than focusing on getting Mindy to try to hear Kirk, I had each party look at their own behavior and try to see it more objectively. I had them brainstorm about what ill effects their parenting style might cause.

Mindy identified that giving in to every whim and desire of their children was not the best way to prepare them for the real world. She saw that both her son and daughter were quite entitled around her and did not have the same respect for her that they had for their dad, who was better at saying no. She saw that they manipulated her left and right, which contributed to her feelings of inadequacy as a parent. She was cheating her children out of learning about life on its own terms, and leading them to believe that they should get everything they wanted. She also felt that she had undercut her own self-worth by not setting firm boundaries with her kids.

Kirk saw that the rigid style he portrayed was teaching his children to be perfectionists. He had thought he was teaching them discipline (as his strict father had done for him) but ultimately understood that he was being overly punishing of his children for simply being human. He realized that his kids did not take risks and always chose the safe route in life.

So after all these years, how did this couple have such a drastic shift in thinking? The key for Kirk and Mindy was coming to these realizations on their own. They had tried for years to get each other to listen or understand, to no avail. Because of human nature, when one would try to convince the other, each would get defensive and make less of an effort to hear the other's point of view.

With a few voluntary changes and some patience, both Kirk and Mindy changed their ways and were able to support each other in their new parenting styles, which were closer to the middle of the road. Rather than perpetuating a huge wedge between them, their parenting now brought them closer. When Mindy had a hard time saying no, she actually went to Kirk and asked him for support and advice on how to stand firm. Kirk did the same when he sensed himself being too rigid, seeking out Mindy to learn a more flexible, open-minded approach.

This couple was able to turn around a thirteen-year-long pattern, simply by being willing to look at their behaviors and learn from each other's perspective. It took putting their marriage on the line for them to reach this level of willingness to change, but they were grateful that they could reverse the dynamic before it was too late.

■ *Case Example:* Jeanine and Roger's Story

Jeanine came to me seeking guidance on whether or not to divorce her husband of eighteen years. She loved Roger but was enraged by his lack of earning power and poor investment decisions.

He was a venture capitalist who was always out looking for the next big deal. He earned his money by investing in computer start-up companies. Jeanine used the money she earned to invest in real estate. It seemed that all of her financial choices produced gains, while his created monetary sinkholes. The more she brought in, the more he tried to impress her with his investments. The more he invested, the more he lost, thus the angrier she became, so the more he tried to please her, and so on. For a long time, she made enough money that he could get away with his tactics, but the day came when their combined net income was in the red.

When she came to see me, she simply couldn't take it anymore. She felt that if she stayed with Roger, she would have to go down with the ship, and she resented having to suffer because of his impulsivity and grandiosity (he always had big schemes to earn them millions, which never seemed to pan out).

She also realized that if she left, she would suffer from the mountainous debt he had created, for which she would be held equally responsible (they lived in California, which is a community property state, so debts acquired during marriage are shared 50-50). On top of that, she might even have to provide him with spousal support.

Jeanine said to me tearfully, "If he would just stop making bad financial decisions and listen to me, we wouldn't have to divorce." She was angry that he couldn't or wouldn't see how destructive his behaviors had been.

What we were able to explore in our work together was how she had unconsciously made it okay for him to continue a pattern that hurt them both. Even though, on the surface, she told him what she needed and that she didn't approve of his irresponsible decisions, her actions had given him a different message. In classic codependent style, she had made life easier for him and taken away his consequences. She had also harped on him to the point where his problem was not his finances; it was her.

Jeanine put an end to bailing Roger out. She stopped selling off more assets to fund his bad decisions. She also stopped yelling at him in an attempt to get him to listen to her. Instead, she kept the focus of her energy on herself and her investments.

Like magic, within six months Roger stopped spending his money impulsively. Because Jeanine had stepped back, he was able to see the consequences of his own actions. When the well ran dry, he had no one to blame but himself.

With the additional intervention of a financial counselor, they were able to keep their marriage together and maintain a sense of financial equilibrium and well-being.

These types of stable working partnerships are available to anyone who is willing to put the effort into changing his or her own habits to positively affect the relationship as a whole.

Exercise: Assessing Your Actions and Reactions

Your spouse probably regularly exhibits some behaviors that knock you off balance. How do you react to those behaviors? How would you like to respond differently to your spouse's behavior to create a better dynamic? If you can't think of any new responses on your own, ask others how they might respond.

A. Look at the sample chart below to identify the usual dynamics a couple might engage in, as well as some alternative reactions:

Action/ Reaction Chart	Spouse's behavior: Demanding	Spouse's behavior: Generous	Spouse's behavior: Blaming	Spouse's behavior: Fearful
My usual reaction	compliant	distrustful	defensive	fearful
Other reactions I might have	curious	happy	under-standing	confident
	stubborn	giving	remorseful	caretaking

B. In the following chart, fill in your spouse's behavior that you dislike, then fill in how you normally react. Fill in other ways you could react to the same behavior that might inspire healthier interaction.

Action/ Reaction Chart	Spouse's behavior:	Spouse's behavior:	Spouse's behavior:	Spouse's behavior:
My usual reaction				
Other reactions I might have				

C. In this last chart, fill in your behavior and your spouse's reactions, as well as your preferred reactions from him or her.

Action/ Reaction Chart	My behavior: _____	My behavior: _____	My behavior: _____	My behavior: _____
My spouse's usual reaction				
Other reactions he or she might have				

1. Looking at these actions and reactions, what did you learn about your situation? Can you identify areas where either of you acts or reacts in order to bring balance to the issue or character trait?

2. Is there any aspect of what isn't working in your relationship that you can take responsibility for and change?

As in past exercises, this one can help you become more aware of the many choices you have in how to react in any given circumstance. These options may not come naturally yet, but with practice they certainly can become second nature.

Understanding Others' Viewpoints

You bring your past experience to all your relationships. Your past shapes you and helps determine your current perspective on the world. How you view others and interact with them is directly related to what has happened to you previously in your life. This is true for everyone. Each person has been influenced in a unique way.

This dynamic was clearly played out by Kirk and Mindy, whose parenting styles were directly impacted by what they had been taught. They had similar upbringings, but because Kirk agreed with his rigid family structure, he continued to parent the same way, while Mindy, who disagreed with this method, chose a kinder and softer approach.

There is an exercise that does an excellent job of demonstrating how and why people can have such disparate perceptions and reactions to the same event. If a group of people sits in a circle around a piece of paper that has a drawing resembling a loose letter "M," and are asked what they see, everyone will say something different depending on where he or she is sitting in the circle. One person may respond that she sees an "M." Another may see a mountain range, and another, a bird flying through the sky, while someone else may see a "W" or a "3." The different responses can go on and on. The point is, depending on your perspective, you see events differently than someone else might. It is tempting to assume that the other person is wrong, but rather than jump to that conclusion, it may be more useful to ask that person how and why he or she sees things that way. You might learn a great deal about the person, while broadening your own horizons.

The way this plays out in your marriage is that you and your spouse see life from two distinct perspectives: yours is based on your past experience, and your spouse's is based on his or her previous life experience.

Exercise: Taking a Poll

A. Using the letter "M" exercise above, can you think of examples of how you and your spouse view the world differently? If you attempted to view life more from your spouse's perspective, would that help you better understand your current interpersonal dynamic?

B. Another version of understanding how differently people view things in life is to ask four or five people how they would react to the following four scenarios. Compare all the answers and see how distinct each person's response is.

1. What (or whom) do you think of when watching a football game? Why?

2. How would you react if someone said that you were fat? Why?

3. How would you react if someone driving in the next lane suddenly hit your car? Why?

4. How would you react if someone asked you to get in front of a group from your neighborhood and say a few words about what you perceive to be the problems in your area and how they need to be fixed? Why?

What you will find is that each person answering likely has a different response from yours and those of the other respondents. Others may give several answers that you never would have thought of, because they were so far outside your realm of experience. For example, men's responses are likely to differ greatly from women's. Different generations may also respond differently. Culture and religion factor into each person's perception, as does simply having different life experiences than another person has.

In a previous exercise, "Assessing Your Actions and Reactions," you learned that changing your reaction to a situation influences the interpersonal dynamics. You may resist taking responsibility by continuing to look outside yourself for the answers (for example, trying to change your spouse, so you can feel better), but you will eventually come to terms with the futility of that strategy. You can only change yourself and your response to other people and situations. (Refer to the suggested reading list for books on relationship dynamics.)

Because it takes so much courage to really look at *your part* in the relationship, I consider this work to be advanced psychotherapy. Your willingness and ability to examine yourself and change old ways of thinking and reacting will bring positive changes to your life.

Willingness Is Key

It can be extremely challenging to break out of old ways of relating to yourself and the world around you. You have to be willing to take a good, hard look at yourself and sit with the discomfort that comes from choosing a new behavior. However, when you begin to see how much you can change the dynamics in all of your relationships, you will experience the rewards that these changes can bring.

I hope that reading this chapter has helped you gain an understanding of some of your outdated beliefs and ways of relating. I hope you are willing and able to heal your old wounds and see where your life and marriage are out of balance. While you can't change anyone but yourself, altering your actions and reactions can't help but influence the people around you.

5

Knowing What You Need

Your vision will become clear only when you look into your heart.

—Carl Gustav Jung

Like it or not, you have needs; we all do. We would hardly be human if we didn't. In my work, I am often surprised by how many people, men and women alike, either try to deny their needs or don't know they have them. These unmet needs are the leading underlying factors behind most disputes and disappointments couples have. The more disputes and disappointments you have, the more tumultuous your relationship, and therefore, the more likely you are to divorce.

Gaining clarity on identifying your personal and marital needs, as well as how and where to get your needs met, has a huge impact on the direction you take in your marriage. Once you know and understand your needs, you can take action to help your spouse meet them. Whatever issues caused the problems can be addressed. However, for some, uncovering your needs may hasten the realization that your spouse is unwilling or incapable of meeting them.

When people have unmet needs in their marriage, they either go without and suffer or get their needs met somewhere else. As you will see later in this chapter, it's not realistic or even healthy to expect your spouse to meet all of your needs; however, going outside the marriage for sex, for example, is almost always destructive.

What's Wrong with Having Needs?

What is it about having needs that has such negative implications? Since we all have them, why can't we be more open about our needs with ourselves and others? What's the big deal?

Well, by virtue of having needs, we are rendered vulnerable, a state most of us feel uncomfortable being in. If our physical needs aren't met, we can literally die. In the realm of our emotional needs, we may not die if they are left unfulfilled, but we are subject to being deeply wounded and feeling tremendous pain or sadness.

We are often dependent on others to help us satisfy our needs. This is especially true in childhood, when we are the most dependent we will ever be. How well our childhood needs were met and what we were taught about needing and being needed set the stage for the rest of our lives. The next section will help you look at the role your needs play in your everyday life.

Hierarchy of Needs

Abraham Maslow, a twentieth-century psychologist, developed what he called a *hierarchy of needs*, a series of needs that he believed motivated us on a day-to-day basis (1943a, 370–396). Maslow postulated that these needs are progressive in the sense that you cannot advance to the next level of need until your more basic needs are met. In observing chimpanzees, Maslow noticed significant behavior changes depending on the level of the need: the more survival-based the need, the more agitated, aggressive, or even violent the behavior of those seeking fulfillment of their needs. The more advanced the need, the more interrelational and cooperative the behavior. Maslow saw that there was more of a sense of urgency in getting the lowest needs met (as if their lives depended on it, which they did), whereas when the primates could focus on their higher needs, they operated from a calmer, more trusting, and cooperative place. Maslow then translated these observations to humans and found that the same patterns held true.

FIGURE 6: HIERARCHY OF NEEDS

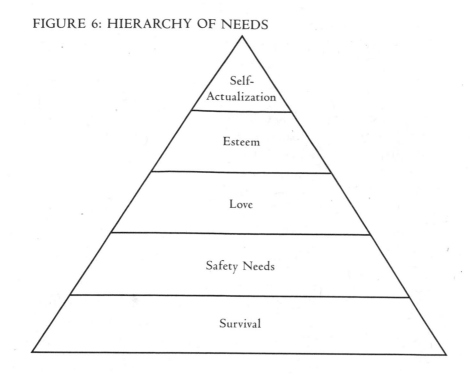

From the Bottom to the Top

When our basic human needs go unmet, we become more pushy, aggressive, and fearful. When we feel safe, comfortable, loved, and esteemed, we tend to have more confidence and ease, trusting that we will continue getting whatever we need.

Maslow identifies the four lower needs as the *deficiency needs*, those that *must* be met, while the fifth need is considered a *growth need*, one that's less vital for our survival as humans but plays a major role in shaping our behavior.

Starting at the foundation of the pyramid, we can see that our most basic needs are for water and food. Without the right balance of each of these requirements, we would die. Most of us in the world today hardly give these needs a thought, but if we were rendered homeless in a natural disaster, for example, getting these needs met would be our primary concern.

Once we have our physiological needs met, we can then focus on our safety needs by obtaining security and protection. It would not help our survival if we had a protective structure around us without food or water, but the opposite is not true. For example, we can usually survive without feeling safe and secure as long as we have enough to eat and drink. We aren't necessarily happy or comfortable, but we will not die from lack of such amenities.

With our physical needs tended to, we are then able to focus on our needs to be loved and to belong. This is followed by our esteem needs, which include not only having self-esteem but also being esteemed and respected by those around us.

The final need at the top of the list is self-actualization. Maslow describes self-actualized people as able to deal with life on life's terms (reality-based), accepting of themselves and others, flexible in thoughts and actions, and solution oriented.

Maslow also observed that self-actualized people are open minded, and can act and think independently of social and cultural influences they may have been raised with. Finally, he noted that these people have a deep appreciation for all of the people in their lives and for all of their experiences.

In short, self-actualized people have their most basic needs met and can therefore focus on continued self-improvement as well as giving back to their communities or the world.

Marriage and the Hierarchy of Needs

This section examines marriage as the living organism that it is, a separate entity with needs of its own. Breaking it down into various components or levels of need may make it easier for you to identify which levels you and your spouse primarily operate on, and what you need to keep your marriage alive and help it thrive.

Just how does a marriage survive? What must be present for both spouses to feel safe? How do both get their love needs met? And we can ask the same questions about how both get their esteem and actualization needs met within the marriage.

While some answers may differ from couple to couple, most people in most cultures would agree that certain basic qualities must be present in a marriage. Chapter 6 explores these needs as they apply to particular situations you may encounter in your marriage, but by way of introduction, the marital hierarchy of needs breaks down as follows:

Marriage Survival Needs

You must be legally married (in the eyes of the state or church), have a mutual agreement to be married, and live in the same house or at least have regular contact with your spouse. In survival mode you don't have to love or even like your spouse to have a marriage; you simply need to maintain your status as married.

Marriage Safety Needs

To feel safe with each other, you take care of and provide comfort to one another; create a home; establish financial security; have mutual trust and honesty; protect one another physically, mentally, and emotionally; and maintain an abuse-free environment within the marriage.

Marriage Love Needs

Mutual love is an obvious requirement to have a marriage that operates from this level. Kindness, compassion, companionship, intimacy, affection, and sex (lovemaking) are also important factors here.

Marriage Esteem Needs

To reach this level, you need to have self-esteem and esteem from your spouse, as well as mutual respect and the ability to honor commitments.

Marriage Actualization Needs

Because the lower needs have been met, one or both spouses can support the other to reach their respective goals; each can sacrifice his or her own needs (to a healthy degree) for the bigger picture; both interact maturely; both maintain a healthy balance in life; each feels a sense of fulfillment in life; and both give back to the community.

We have all been taught that love is the only requirement for a relationship to work, and as a society we often focus on maintaining this love. But what we are not taught is that we must feed, water, and nurture our marriage by meeting the lower needs of the union. Assuming, as Maslow does, that you can't get to a higher level without having the lower needs met, how would a marriage look if its lower needs went unsatisfied? Can a marriage be sustained in such a situation? The following example will give you an idea.

■ *Case Example:* Logan and Monica's Story

When Logan was just fifteen years old, he already knew that he wanted to marry his classmate Monica someday. He simply adored her. It took him a year to build up the nerve to ask her out, but when he did, she was thrilled. They dated for two years and married immediately after high-school graduation.

Neither had any direction or idea of what careers they might want to pursue but felt strongly that their mutual love would pull them through. They found an apartment complex and became the building superintendents, which significantly reduced their monthly rent.

Logan went to work at a local department store, while Monica enrolled in a college program to study environmental sciences. Although the tuition was relatively inexpensive, Logan's income wasn't enough to cover rent, tuition, food, and basic living expenses, so he decided to get a second job to bring home more pay.

For the first four years of their marriage while Monica was in school, this young couple barely scraped by financially. They lived at the edge of poverty and in constant fear of not having enough. Just when Monica was about to graduate and get a job to help bring in more money, she became pregnant. If their monetary status had been better, they might have been happy to have a child, but instead they felt defeated, as if they could never get ahead.

Monica took a part-time job during her pregnancy but quit working when she gave birth to their son. For the next two years, she stayed at home with the baby.

At this point, they were six years into their marriage and still struggling to make ends meet. The financial stress on the marriage was what brought them in to see me. They fought incessantly, and were now considering separating and living with their respective parents to save some money and get a stronger foundation underneath them.

There was no trust or sense of safety between them. Monica blamed Logan for their money troubles, and he blamed her. They both agreed that they needed a break from each other and that it was hard to know whether they still had feelings of love for each other because they had functioned from such a raw survival mode for so long. They had never known a life together without their survival and safety needs being threatened. They figured that if they could get back to a place of feeling strong financially, they would be able to tell if there were still any feelings of love.

The good news for Monica and Logan was that they eventually took their parents up on the offer to help. As a result, they were able to improve their financial situation, and within a year they moved back in together. Monica secured a full-time job at a local environmental organization, and Logan was able to enroll in some computer vocational classes while working part-time. Because Monica's mother had retired, she was happy to provide free child care to her grandson, which was an immense relief to the couple.

Given that Monica and Logan had been on the edge all the time, they couldn't be certain they would survive, and didn't feel safe. Their love, while present, was not a priority. They couldn't focus on it, because their survival needs were threatened all the time. Because this young couple was able to rely on their families of origin, they got stronger, but many people don't have this option.

So, the answer to the question of whether you can sustain a marriage if the lower needs go unmet is yes. However, the quality of the marriage will suffer as a result. If your marriage is operating without a solid foundation, it can probably survive, but it (and you) will definitely not thrive.

Exercise: Marriage Needs Assessment

Using the knowledge you just gained about what a marriage needs to stay alive and subsequently flourish, see if you can identify which needs are being met in your marriage, which are not being met, and what you can do to remedy the relationship. Check all of the boxes that apply to your situation:

1. Which of the basic survival needs does your marriage meet?
    - ☐ You are legally married.
    - ☐ You have an agreement to be married.
    - ☐ You live together and/or have regular contact.

2. Which safety needs does your marriage meet?
    - ☐ You feel safe with each other.
    - ☐ You take care of and provide comfort to one another.

☐ You create a home.

☐ You have financial security.

☐ You share mutual trust.

☐ You have mutual honesty.

☐ You protect one another physically, mentally, and emotionally.

☐ You maintain an abuse-free environment within the marriage.

3. Which love needs does your marriage meet?

☐ You share mutual love for each other.

☐ You share companionship.

☐ You share kindness and compassion.

☐ You share intimacy, affection, and sex (lovemaking).

4. Which esteem needs does your marriage meet?

☐ You have self-esteem and esteem for your spouse.

☐ You have mutual respect.

☐ You both honor your commitments to each other.

5. Which actualization needs does your marriage meet?

☐ You support each other to reach respective goals.

☐ You maintain a healthy balance in life.

☐ You feel a sense of fulfillment in your life.

☐ You give back to the community.

6. In what areas are your marital needs going unmet?

7. What level would you say your marriage operates from most of the time?

8. Are higher-level needs being met while lower-level needs go unmet? If so, how does this impact your relationship? (For example, you have a tumultuous relationship, you love but don't trust your spouse, or you can't be as intimate as you would like.)

9. What can you (or both of you) do to meet the lower needs of your marriage and consistently function at a higher level?

10. If there is something that needs to change but is out of your control to change it, what other resources can you call on to improve your marriage?

In viewing your marriage as the living organism that it is, you have probably just seen your relationship in a completely new light. Write in your journal about any realizations you have had as a result of doing this exercise.

Knowing What You Need

You have needs; your spouse has needs; if you have kids, they have needs; and your marriage has needs. This is a lot to juggle. It's much easier to focus on one or two of these needy entities, and if you are like most people, you have ignored your own needs and those of your marriage to take care of your kids' and spouse's needs.

It makes sense that you can't get what you need if you don't ask for it but can't ask for it if you don't know what you need. I'm amazed by how many people have no inkling what their own physical, mental, and emotional needs are, never mind those of their marriage. Often, these folks are overly focused on their spouses' or children's needs, and consider it a luxury or even selfish to worry about their own needs or those of the marriage.

For those of you who are parents, part of your job is to meet your children's needs; while it *is* appropriate for spouses to look out for each other's needs, problems arise when you forego *your* individual needs to meet your children's and spouse's needs.

I suggest that you get better at identifying your needs, and make sure your needs show up in the top two or three entries of your daily to-do list. Otherwise, you will get lost in the shuffle, which sets you up to feel resentful and neglected.

The following story illustrates how being unaware of your needs and solely serving others can interfere with all of your relationships.

■ *Case Example:* Sarah's Story

Sarah, a woman in her late forties, was a new member of my Relationship Insight group. She joined the group after her divorce was final, expressing that there were certain patterns she and her ex had fallen into that she didn't fully understand and didn't want to repeat. A dynamic she recognized was that she always gave in to other people's needs and wants, but didn't know why.

One day she called and was frantic to come in to see me. She said that she was having an anxiety attack and hoped I could help calm her down.

In the session, she immediately conveyed that she could trace her panicky feelings to a current situation. Her boyfriend planned to stay with her and her two daughters, which the girls (aged sixteen and eighteen) were unhappy about. Sarah said that she always became anxious whenever she felt that she was making someone else unhappy, especially her kids. At the same time, she had a small voice within her that confirmed her right to spend time with her boyfriend without being punished for it.

I asked Sarah why her children would have a problem with her spending time with her new boyfriend, and she responded that it could be because this was her first relationship since her divorce. It made sense that she would have some fear and anxiety in exploring this new territory, but it seemed to me that there was more to it than that.

Next, I asked Sarah to talk about what her parents had modeled for her in getting their own needs met and what they had taught her about having needs. Immediately, Sarah told me that when she was only seven years old, her mother had announced to her, her sister, and her father that she was moving a thousand miles away and that, while she would always be their mom, she needed to go take care of herself and stop caring for everyone else around her. Sarah also remembered her mother telling her not to cry or be upset and to be a good girl for her father.

Given that, as a seven-year-old, Sarah didn't have the capacity to understand what may have really been behind her mother's need to leave (regardless of whether the cause was burnout from being a mom, meeting someone new, or a nervous breakdown), she assumed that her mother was leaving because she had done something wrong or bad.

In Sarah's immature mind, she had decided that she would be a "good girl" and do as her mother had instructed. She never cried about her mother's leaving, even though it was quite devastating for her. At that young age, Sarah began to suppress her own needs and feelings.

Sarah had observed that when her mother took care of her own needs, everyone else around her suffered. In turn, Sarah came to believe that having needs of her own would hurt others. Instead, she dedicated herself to understanding and meeting others' needs (it's no mystery why she became a doctor). Well into her adulthood, Sarah still held her child-hood belief that if she focused on meeting everyone else's needs, they would always love her and never leave her.

As she uncovered the layers of this faulty belief system, Sarah noticed that her anxiety emerged not only in situations where she didn't stand up for herself but also whenever one of her own needs simply bubbled up. The clenching in her gut was an unconscious tool she had developed to squelch her needs.

Sarah had learned how to shut down that small voice before it ever saw the light of day. She had done this for so many years that it had become a built-in mechanism, and she was unaware that there was another way of being.

It was extremely challenging for her to stand up to her children, boyfriend, parents, and friends, but she began to practice checking in with herself to discern her needs so she could then articulate her needs to others. Within six months, she had become a new woman, with a much more balanced life. It was no longer about sacrificing herself to serve others. She realized that there was a lot more room for her to get what she needed than she had ever thought possible and that no one was hurt as a result.

Sarah eventually understood that putting her children's needs ahead of her own taught them that her needs didn't matter. It also set them up to have unrealistic expectations of her and the rest of the world.

On a bittersweet note, Sarah also saw that, had she prioritized her own needs sooner in her life, she might not have had to get divorced. She felt at peace with how things eventually turned out and was able to take responsibility for one important aspect of why the marriage had not worked out.

The type of unmet needs that Sarah had were primarily her security and love needs. Being wounded as a child when her mother left was an abandonment that prompted Sarah's belief that she would not be taken care of (security needs) and that she was not loved or loveable (love needs). The notion that if Sarah had needs, she would be left and that it was her job to serve others' needs set her up to do everything for everyone without asking anything in return.

Sarah believed that her marriage had ended because she had ignored her own needs. Learning from this gave her the ability to head off problems in her current situation with her children and boyfriend by acknowledging her own needs.

The Three-Step Guide to Getting Your Needs Met

It can take years to gain enough life experience and self-assurance to identify your needs and give yourself permission to expose these needs to others. I have found a three-step process that can help people get their needs met. While the process may sound simple, it isn't always easy to implement, especially for those who, like Sarah, were taught that it was wrong to even have needs.

This three-step process consists of (1) acknowledging that you have needs, (2) clearly identifying your needs, and (3) learning how and where to get your needs met. Couples who practice these tools together can't help but communicate better and experience a healthier relationship. Dynamics can certainly improve when just one partner implements these steps, though it is a bit more challenging. As we saw with Sarah, she possibly would not have had to get divorced had she known about these tools.

Acknowledging That You Have Needs

Children aren't the only ones who need to feel acknowledged; we all do. It's not unlike when you've had a hard day and tell someone about it. Often, the mere process of venting about the events that went wrong makes you feel better. When the person listening conveys a similar experience or says the exact thing you needed to hear, it is even better. You feel heard and understood. The problem may remain, but your desire to dwell on it vanishes. You can let it go.

Your needs operate in much the same way as a child tugging at your sleeve, trying to get your attention. Once you recognize your needs and allow them to be there, they no longer need to run the show.

When you feel an internal tug from something calling for your attention—whether it's about something you need from your spouse, the need to take a time-out for yourself, or the need for a friend's advice—if you can listen to that urging and honor it, the need will actually dissipate, and you will almost always feel better. It's when you ignore your needs or put them at the end of the list and save them for the day's end (when they're less likely to get met sufficiently, if at all) that you feel resentful, depressed, or anxious. It's as if that inner child, the part of you that needs something, is having a tantrum, bubbling up to try to get you to pay attention.

Exercise: How Do You Handle Having Needs?

This exercise helps you explore how you feel about having needs and how you deal with your needs when they arise.

1. How do you feel about having needs?

2. Discuss how you treat yourself when you feel a need emerge.

3. Can you identify ways in which you have put the needs of your family (spouse and children) before your own needs? If so, how have you done that?

4. Why have you put your family's needs before your own?

5. Is there anything inside you needing your attention and acknowledgment? If so, can you identify what it is? You will often feel a physical symptom; for example, you get sick to your stomach, feel a panic attack coming on, get headaches, or suddenly feel very tired.

6. What, if anything, can you do today to better acknowledge your own needs?

As you improve at identifying your needs and asking to have them met, I encourage you to revisit this exercise. I hope that you will find it easier and easier to expose your vulnerabilities to others and call in whatever support you need, when you need it. If this has not been your norm, you will find it challenging to begin this practice, but the benefits will absolutely outweigh the discomfort you may experience.

Clearly Identifying Your Needs

In acknowledging your internal messages, you realize that you *have* a need. The next step is getting clear about *what* you need. Clearly identifying what you need in any area of your life can be the single most powerful step you can take toward improving your circumstances. Once you know what you need, you have a better sense of what direction to take in your marriage, and know what to ask for. Gaining this clarity is not always easy, but it is a vital component of getting your needs met.

In my work with couples, I always try to get to the bottom-line need of each partner. When both are clear about their individual needs, they can begin asking for support from one another (or someone else) to get their needs met.

■ *Case Example:* Lowell and Sharon's Story

I recently met with Lowell and Sharon for a series of counseling sessions. They had been married for over twenty years and didn't really know why they were consulting me or what they needed. They had tossed around the "D" word in recent conversations, but at least initially neither seemed sure whether that option was actually on the table.

What became evident to me relatively quickly was that each had distinct needs, but neither could communicate about them. Additionally, each spouse seemed to demand that the other meet his or her needs, even though the needs of each remained unclear. It was a nightmare!

In our first several sessions, I felt as if I were undoing a succession of snarls. I had to gingerly help them unravel the confusing misconnection in one area to get to the crossed wires in another. By creating an intricate web of miscommunication, destruction, and even deception, this couple had become lost in a maze of pain. Much of this maze resulted from their unacknowledged and unexpressed needs.

We finally sifted through enough layers to discover that both spouses felt tremendous fear. Lowell expressed that he felt unneeded and unloved by Sharon. He considered Sharon extremely competitive and felt that she always tried to win the kids' love, beat him at earning money, and put him down any way she could so that she could feel better about herself.

Lowell kept one foot out the door, because he didn't want to stay married under these circumstances. At the same time, he feared that he would have to remain in this marriage for the rest of his life. He worried that Sharon would punish him by using the children as pawns if they divorced. No matter which way he turned, Lowell felt that Sharon could and would hurt him, if given a chance.

On the other hand, Sharon did need Lowell, but because she never told him her specific needs, he often disappointed her. She realized that she had been afraid to express her needs to Lowell for fear that he would regard her as weak. Sharon felt that she needed to stay strong, and eventually acknowledged that the reason she put Lowell down was that she wanted him to depend upon her. Knowing that Lowell was unhappy in their relationship, Sharon's biggest fear was that he would leave her to raise their three teenage children by herself. She needed the security of knowing that he would stay and work on the marriage with her and not abandon her.

Before entering couples therapy, both spouses had been reluctant to be honest with one another. Instead, they had clouded over their truths with blame, confusion, and surface-level distractions. Once they got to the bottom of the tension, they saw that both needed to feel needed, secure, and honored. Each had different ways of pushing to get his or her needs met and feel heard, but because both were so unaware of their real needs, they acted out in ways that hurt each other. It's no wonder that they fought all the time.

What ultimately happened was that Lowell agreed to hang in there for another nine months to see if Sharon could honor and respect him enough to make it worth staying in the marriage. He felt willing to try this, with the knowledge that if things didn't improve for him, they would then implement a trial separation. We also addressed his need to not feel punished if he left.

During the nine-month period, Sharon got a clear picture of what it would look like for Lowell to be a supportive co-parent. Although at times she felt his threat of leaving hanging over her, she understood that it was important to practice clearly communicating what she needed from him, regardless of whether or not they stayed together. In particular, they addressed her need to be more supported by Lowell.

Although both Lowell and Sharon learned a tremendous amount about what it really means to be in a marriage (for example, communicating clearly and taking responsibility for your own needs), after the nine months passed, they decided to go their separate ways.

But now they had a solid co-parenting plan in place, and both understood that their pattern of staying confused and blaming each other had perpetuated a destructive dynamic. Instead of continuing to employ the knee-jerk pattern of making the other wrong, each was able to learn to go within and assess what he or she truly needed. By gaining this clarity, they were able to stop trying to manipulate each other to meet their needs, and eventually found other people and means to get their needs met.

Exercise: Are You Clearly Asking for What You Need?

As you saw in Lowell and Sharon's story, sometimes the reason people don't meet your needs is that you have not clearly let them know what you need. This exercise invites you to go a bit deeper to honestly assess what more you can do to be direct and honest in asking for your needs to be met.

1. Have you clearly communicated your needs to yourself and your spouse?

2. List one to three areas of your marriage in which you need something from your spouse that you are not getting (for example, parenting support, help around the house, or affection).

_____   _____   _____

3. Do you directly ask for what you need? If not, why not?

4. What are some ways you can use clear and direct communication to get these needs met?

Clearly asking for what you need is one of those tasks that, if it is against your nature to be direct, can take a while to do and do well, but it is an important skill to learn and will assist you in all of your interpersonal relationships.

Knowing How and Where to Get Your Needs Met

As humans, we all have certain needs in common, but there are variations on what our needs consist of. Children have different needs than do teens, who have different needs than adults do. Single people have far different needs than do couples. People from one culture may have different needs than people from another.

Perhaps the most pertinent example of differing needs is that of men and women. We all know the gender archetypes (introduced in John Gray's well-known work) that men are from Mars, and women from Venus. And for years we've heard about the very real physiological differences between the way men process thoughts and feelings, and the way women do. The bottom line is that we are wired differently and don't share exactly the same set of needs. The lack of understanding and acceptance of this one factor has contributed greatly to the demise of many a relationship.

Often, the divorcing women I've worked with admit that they tried to lean on their husbands as they did their best girlfriends. These women got mad and frustrated when their husbands didn't seem to understand their need to just be heard. They would complain, "He didn't listen," "He only offered solutions to my problems," or "He didn't reciprocate by telling me about his day." The men I've counseled have also realized that they have made some of their worst mistakes by assuming that their wives had the same set of needs as they had.

It's not enough to recognize that you have needs and to understand your needs. To have your needs fulfilled, you have to know where and how to get them met. If you continue going to the hardware store for bread, as they say, you will continue to feel disappointed and frustrated, and be no closer to getting your loaf of bread. In fact, consistently going to the wrong source to get your needs fulfilled can leave you feeling worse than if you had never reached out.

Many people look to their spouses to meet all of their needs. This brings us back to the point in chapter 2 found in Stephanie Coontz's observation that, in more recent times, couples have begun leaning too heavily on each other to satisfy all their needs and wants. It is part of the romantic and unrealistic ideals of being swept away by Prince Charming or taken care of by the doting wife.

KNOWING WHO CAN MEET YOUR NEEDS

So, how do you know where to go to get your needs met? The best place to start is by looking within. Once you have clearly identified your need, you can ask yourself if you have the knowledge, resources, or experience to meet this need on your own. I once had a supervisor who trained me to do whatever I could to find the answer myself rather than immediately go to him for the answer. I learned quite a bit more than if he had handed me the information, and also remembered it better.

Next, you can ask others to meet your needs. Your spouse may be a good place to start, especially if your need has to do with your relationship or immediate family. However, if you can't clearly communicate what you need or have tried repeatedly to get your spouse to meet this need to no avail, he or she may not be able to give it to you. At this stage your options are to back up a step and communicate your need more clearly or accept that your spouse may be incapable of meeting your need. To keep asking or making your spouse feel wrong for not meeting you on your level does not make for a peaceful relationship. Lowell and Sharon's story illustrates this dynamic well. Although they ended up separating, I have seen many people who were able to fulfill their partners' needs and change the dynamic while maintaining their marriages.

Other resources for getting what you need can include friends and family. Most people enjoy feeling useful and being of service and don't feel imposed upon when you ask for help with something.

Doctors, lawyers, therapists, clergy, and coaches are examples of professional resources you can consult for assistance with a variety of areas in your life, from physical well-being to mental and emotional needs to spiritual needs.

Trial and error is indispensable for discerning the right resources for your particular situation. Try one way to get what you need, and if that doesn't work, you can either give it another shot or move on to a different approach. It's important to be willing to make mistakes and move on if it's not working.

■ *Case Example:* Nancy's Story

I had a client, named Nancy, who was trying to pass the bar exam to become an attorney, which had been her lifelong dream. After failing the exam twice, she was about to take it for the third time. One day she came to me in tears because her husband, Jake, was driving her crazy with advice. When she sought solace from him about the challenges of taking the bar exam, he responded, "Just go get a tutor" or "Just study the material more." These comments enraged her, because he had no comprehension of the depth and breadth of material she needed to know, nor did he understand that you couldn't just go hire a tutor.

When I suggested that she lean on law school friends for support and stop talking to Jake about the bar exam, her jaw dropped. She said, "You mean that's okay? I don't have to tell Jake about my difficulties with the exam?" It never would have crossed her mind to go to someone other than her husband for support in any area of her life, because in her mind, that was what marriage was all about, supporting each other in every endeavor.

I explained to her that it would be fine to seek his advice if he were giving her what she needed but that was not the case here. Nancy had told Jake about her difficulties, and he had tried to help her by coming up with what seemed like logical solutions. She had gotten upset and said, "You don't understand. It's not that simple!" In turn, he had felt rejected and had become angry and frustrated with her. Nancy went on to reveal that the couple had fought more in the past month than in their entire five years of marriage.

I suggested that she just let Jake know that this topic was off-limits for them from now on. A week later, Nancy called and profusely thanked me. She reported that they had both agreed to stop talking about the bar exam, and miraculously, the fighting had stopped.

Exercise: How and Where Do You Get Your Needs Met?

This exercise is a quick inventory to assess how, where, and with whom you get your needs met.

1. How do you usually get your survival and safety needs met? (For example, my parents, my spouse, my job.)

2. How do you usually get your love and esteem needs met? (For example, my friends, my spouse, my career.)

3. How do you get your actualization needs met? (For example, by volunteering at my kid's school, by serving on a local nonprofit board.)

4. Which of your needs do you meet on your own?

5. What needs does your spouse meet well for you?

6. In looking at the needs you ask your spouse to fulfill, how important is it to you that your spouse meet those needs? Are there other people or places you could turn to for meeting these needs?

7. What needs do your friends meet?

8. What needs might be better fulfilled from consulting professionals?

Do you notice a pattern in the types of needs your spouse meets for you and vice versa? Do you notice certain needs that you turn to others for that perhaps your spouse should meet? Write your observations in your journal, including your feelings about these patterns.

Knowing What Gets in the Way

Even when you follow the three-step process of acknowledging your needs, clearly identifying your needs, and learning how and where to get your needs met, you still may come away empty. A major reason why many people (especially wives and mothers) don't get their needs met is the habit I mentioned earlier: putting their own needs at the bottom of the to-do list.

By the time these people get around to looking at their own needs, they are too exhausted to do anything for themselves or even ask for assistance. It's crucial to balance your needs with the needs of those around you. And it takes a vigilance to keep your needs high on the list. You cannot give what you don't have, and it's a disservice to all involved parties to take care of everyone and everything around you while ignoring your own needs.

A client of mine explained it this way to her children: "We spend lots of time on your events, and I need to spend some time on my events too." Her children immediately understood and stopped trying to make her feel guilty for not devoting 100 percent of her time and energy to them.

Exercise: What Gets in the Way

In continuing to assess why your needs are or aren't being met, answer the following questions about what real or imagined obstacles might be getting in the way.

1. Make a list of three to six needs you look to your spouse to meet that he or she meets (for example, financial security, intimacy, and co-parenting):

   _____   _____   _____

   _____   _____   _____

2. How have you acknowledged these needs within yourself? With your spouse?

3. How have you tried to meet these needs yourself? With your spouse?

4. How has your spouse responded to your having these needs?

5. What obstacles get in the way of your getting your needs met?

6. Are you aware of having any needs that you don't want to acknowledge? If so, what are they?

7. Why don't you want to acknowledge these needs? What are you avoiding?

8. How can you get support to acknowledge these needs?

9. Are you aware of currently holding any resentment toward your spouse? If so, why?

10. Is this resentment caused by your spouse's unwillingness or inability to meet your needs, or from your inability to express your needs to your spouse?

I hope that this exercise demonstrates that you have more power in getting your needs met than you may have been aware of. As a result, I hope that you feel empowered to make any necessary changes within yourself or your relationships to live a more satisfying life.

Your Marriage and Your Needs

Knowing what you need, how to get it, and what gets in the way of meeting your needs are vital components in understanding how your relationship works. Realizing what level your marriage operates from can be quite illuminating as to why you feel unsatisfied and unfulfilled, or why you want to stay in the relationship.

In a typical marriage, most people take for granted that their lower needs for survival, safety, and love will be met. In a happy marriage, self-esteem may improve, and in a high-functioning nuptial relationship, each person may go out into the world and make the world a better place; each partner feels supported appropriately in all of the lower-level needs.

As long as you get the support you need, does the one supporting you always need to be your spouse? Well, as we saw with Nancy's story, the answer is no. Having said that, there are areas of your life where it is important and appropriate for you to get support from your partner. So the better question to pose is, if you have asked and given your spouse a chance to respond, but he or she cannot (or will not) fulfill your basic marital needs, should you stay in your marriage? This is rarely simply a yes-or-no question. Hopefully, you have a sense of how to answer this question based on what you learned in chapter 3 and in the exercises you have just completed.

To take this question a step further, if your spouse not only fails to meet you halfway but also actually *causes* problems and distress for you, it is especially important to examine your motives for remaining married, and ask yourself whether you are staying for the right reasons.

Divorce and the Hierarchy of Needs

By now, you have a better understanding of the different levels of need you operate from, as well as a better idea of your personal and marital needs. You know which needs your marriage meets (and should meet) and which needs have to be met outside the marriage. You also know how to identify any obstacles that have been in the way of meeting your needs.

One of the most important considerations to make when contemplating divorce is how to meet your needs if you dissolve the marriage. In such circumstances, you may have noticed that primarily your physiological, safety, and love needs seem to be threatened. You may fear that, if your marriage splits up, you will no longer have enough money or resources to get by, to the point of imagining yourself as a homeless person living on the street or being alone without love for the rest of your life. Using an irrational but understandable thought process, many people equate divorce with no money, no food, no protection, no home base, and no love. Just the idea of divorce can trigger many of these core-level fears.

Why does this happen at the mere mention of the word "divorce"? Well, for one thing, the majority of people do experience a decline in discretionary funds, because there are two households to support instead of one. Often one or both spouses have to move out of the home, necessitating selling the house, and the kids have to go without many of the extras, such as sports, music lessons, and tutoring. In addition, the process of divorce itself is expensive and can cut into whatever assets a family has.

It is not uncommon for divorcing individuals to undergo a drastic change in lifestyle, primarily due to the financial changes that divorce brings. Over the years studies have shown that, postdivorce, a woman's standard of living goes down by between 27 and 30 percent, while a man's goes up by 10 percent (Lee 1996), but both parties usually slide backward financially, at least initially. Monetary changes such as these can't help but impact your sense of survival and safety.

Divorce will compromise your need for love and belonging since you will end your shared life with your spouse. In nine out of ten of the cases I have seen, there is still a significant amount of love between husband and wife. It's quite normal to feel sad over losing this relationship, as well as lonely and afraid that you will never meet anyone again. Your need for love will probably be one of the factors that will weigh most heavily in your decision to stay or go, because it is what propelled you to marry in the first place.

Some divorcing individuals grapple with feelings of low self-esteem. They express the belief that they have failed to make the relationship work, failed to maintain their spouse's love, failed in their own lack of faithfulness, or failed as a parent. These are normal responses to divorce, but despite the fact that there are plenty of anti-divorce factions that encourage this line of thinking, there are other ways to view marital dissolution.

In 2005, when Brad Pitt divorced Jennifer Aniston and then announced that he felt it had been a successful marriage, many were aghast. The question in many people's minds (and perhaps yours, as well) was, if their marriage was so successful, why did he leave? He said that he left because he felt that the relationship was over, that it had run its course. Unfortunately for her, Jennifer didn't want the marriage to end and didn't share Brad's opinion that it was finished.

In any case, it is important to surround yourself with people who support you in finding your own truth and to refrain from being manipulated by the "shoulds," which make up the critical chatter in your head pretending to have your best interest in mind. This is the voice that tells you that no matter what you do, it isn't good enough or right; it's similar to an internal scolding parent.

When you become aware of whether you're hearing a loving voice that calls you forward or a scolding voice that tries to keep you down, you can decide whether or not to listen to that voice. Understanding which of your needs pull you to stay in your marriage or push you to leave will help you immensely in your decision-making process so that you can make a more conscious choice.

Exercise: Addressing Your Worst Fears

The fears encountered in divorce contemplation are almost always based on believing that your needs won't be met. Sometimes these fears are based in reality, but often they are not. This exercise asks you to write out some of your fears, followed by some actions you can take to address each of them. There certainly may be some fears that you cannot do anything about, but in most cases you will see steps that you can take to meet your needs.

A. Complete the following sentences to uncover what fears may be present.

If I get divorced…

1. I will be _____.

2. I'm afraid that _____.

3. People will think that _____.

4. My children will _____.

5. I'll never be able to _____.

6. My family will _____.

7. My spouse's family will _____.

8. My friends will _____.

9. _____.

10. _____.

B. Clearly identifying your fears can help you understand what, if anything, you can do to take care of them. Use your answers from section A to come up with a plan to meet or resolve the fears.

If I get divorced…

1. I will be _____. If that happens, I can _____ to resolve it.

2. I'm afraid that _____ . If that happens,
    I can _____ to resolve it.

3. People will think that _____ .
    If that happens, I can _____ to resolve it.

4. My children will _____ .
    If that happens, I can _____ to resolve it.

5. I'll never be able to _____ . If that happens,
    I can _____ to resolve it.

6. My family will _____ . If that happens,
    I can _____ to resolve it.

7. My spouse's family will _____ .
    If that happens, I can _____ to resolve it.

8. My friends will _____ . If that happens,
    I can _____ to resolve it.

9. _____ . If that happens,
    I can _____ to resolve it.

10. _____ . If that happens,
    I can _____ to resolve it.

C. Answer the following questions:

   1. What have you learned from doing this exercise?

   2. Has this changed your opinion about what to do next? If so,
       how?

   I hope that you are now able to see your available resources and understand that you don't have to let fear stop you from moving forward.

Using the knowledge you just gained about your needs, we will explore further what may be keeping you in your marriage. The next two chapters will challenge you to look deeper at your motives. What and whose needs will be met if you remain in your marriage? What would happen to those needs and the people in your life if you left your marriage?

6

Finding Your Truth

We crave and fear becoming truly ourselves.

—Abraham Maslow

As you saw in the previous chapter, your decision to stay or go can be influenced by a multitude of external factors. While you may take these factors into consideration, it is important that you get to *your* bottom-line truth prior to moving ahead.

This chapter will assist you in examining the internal factors that impact your decision so you can further uncover the truth of whether or not your marriage can work out. I have developed guidelines, based on my years of research and experience with relationships, to help you distinguish which marital problems can be worked through and which can't. Knowing what issues can more likely be resolved may help make the decision clearer for you.

I'll challenge you on an even deeper level, by examining not just your *reasons* for contemplating divorce but also the *motives* behind your reasons for staying or going. It can be quite informative to look at what is driving your decision.

Finally, I'll address the all-important issue of a time line. When is staying too long, and when is leaving too soon? This is one of the greatest points of confusion for those contemplating divorce.

It takes courage to be honest with yourself and others. The truth doesn't always feel good and, in fact, can cause pain and heartache. The truth can make life complicated. But, as difficult as honesty can be, deception is always worse and has the potential to create many more heartaches and complications than the truth does. This is why this part of the book challenges you to *thoroughly* examine why you are considering whether or not to stay in your marriage.

If you are considering leaving because your marriage is difficult, and you want a quick fix and think the grass is greener on the other side, I ask you to stay and commit fully until you feel that you have put in the work that your marital commitment deserves. Do everything in your power to work things out with your spouse.

Marriage can be extremely challenging, but if you have not done *everything* you humanly could think of (and could afford) to positively affect the situation, then you are hurting yourself, your spouse, and your marriage. If there is a shadow of doubt whether you have exhausted all avenues, then before taking any action to end your marriage, take more actions to save it. It may take more of your time and money when you feel you can't bear it any longer, but in the big-picture scheme, you will be glad you took those few extra measures to try to work things out.

If you are considering staying because the pain you know seems better than the pain you don't know, it's just easier to stay put, or for any other misguided reason, then I encourage you to challenge your false motives and step out of your comfort zone to find your truth. You are not doing the world any favors by staying in an unhappy situation.

You've arrived at the heart of the book. This is what you've wanted to learn: how to know *if* you should stay in the marriage or leave it, why you should stay or go, and when to follow through with your decision.

Knowing *If* You Should Stay or Go

While there are no quick, easy answers and no "one size fits all" reasons to offer, I will give you parameters within which to gauge whether or not you should remain married to your spouse or leave. I can't give you *your* answer. I can only guide you to find your truth for this moment. Your part will be to follow along and read with honest introspection so you can identify your answer.

When I meet for the first time with a client who is considering divorce, I can often get a sense of whether the scales are tipped toward staying or leaving from the reason he or she gives for wanting to stay married.

If the desire to stay married is based on moving *toward* a goal, the person is more likely to stay married; for example, "I want to raise my children in one house with two parents" or "I want to work on my anger issues and get on the other side of them."

On the other hand, when people explain that they are staying in the marriage to *avoid* pain or fear, this indicates that the marriage hasn't much glue, and such marriages aren't as likely to endure; for instance, "I'm staying because I'm afraid of not seeing my children every day," "I don't know how I'd make ends meet without my spouse," or "No one will ever love me like this again."

Once I hear the reasoning for staying in the marriage, I ask why the client might want to get a divorce. The same rule applies: those who are contemplating leaving to move toward a goal are more likely to actually leave than those who are averting pain or potential consequences. Examples of going toward a goal or away from a fear are "I want more out of life than staying in an unhappy marriage" or "I need to get away from this abuse."

Even though all of these reasons have merit and sound powerful, you may wonder how I know that the person who is moving toward a goal will more likely take action than the one who is running away from or trying to avoid pain. The answer is simple: fear.

Those who are motivated primarily by avoiding pain are usually fear-based people. These people see the world through the eyes of whatever problems and negative repercussions might arise from their actions. They are often imprisoned by their fears, not only as they pertain to deciding whether to stay in or leave their marriages, but in all areas of their lives. These people will more likely stay small, unhappy, and unfulfilled with the thought that they will remain safe.

Action-based people have the opposite view of the world. When they set their sights on a goal, they see what opportunities and benefits might come from moving forward. These people are more willing to take risks and go for what they want. They will also less likely settle for less than what they believe they deserve.

Of course, you can be partially both fear and action based, but whichever mode is dominant will usually win the arguments in your mind about whether to stay or go. The good news is that these aspects are not necessarily set in stone. If you are primarily a fear-based person but would rather be action based, you can push through your fears and accomplish your goals. Most people need some training or support to make these changes, but it is an alteration that anyone can make.

In addition to examining fear-avoidant versus goal-oriented behaviors in the decision-making process, I look at whose needs are driving the decision. In a decision as big as whether or not to stay married, it is imperative that you consider the possible ramifications your leaving may have on others, but *you must also balance that with your own needs.* Where I see people go wrong in such a decision is when they forgo their own needs and focus primarily on meeting the needs of their spouses or children, or, on the contrary, they consider only their own needs and ignore the potential impact on their children and spouses.

■ *Case Example:* Kelly's Story

I spoke with a woman named Kelly about why she wanted to leave her husband. "He's a drunk, he's violent, he yells, he makes us all tense and uptight, he hasn't worked in fifteen years, and he's a miserable SOB!"

Then I asked her why she wanted to stay in the marriage. The answer was, "I'm concerned about money, about having to sell the home, and about the kids. And knowing him, he'll fall apart, and then I'll feel guilty." When I asked her if there was anything about him that made her want to stay in the marriage, she responded that she really couldn't think of anything.

When I asked what they had done to work on the marriage, Kelly revealed that she had tried to get her husband to consult her pastor since he wouldn't see a therapist, but he refused to talk to anyone, declaring that she was the only problem in their marriage.

Kelly's ambivalence about divorcing resulted purely from her fear of the logistics and the impact of splitting up, and had virtually nothing to do with her love for her husband. She did not mention any good side to him. When she had attempted to get outside intervention, he had refused.

In this situation, I would assess (without knowing more about their relationship) that there wasn't much keeping this couple connected. Sure, they shared parenting responsibilities, as well as chores and other responsibilities of running a household, but they had no real conjugal cohesion. It seems as if it should have been a pretty clear decision for Kelly, but she still had a hard time leaving her loveless marriage.

I've had countless clients like Kelly tell me that they don't want to divorce because they are afraid of losing the co-parenting relationship or their spouse's income, only eventually to realize that they alone already carry the load of responsibilities. The spouse doesn't contribute to the marriage but, rather, takes from it.

On awakening to this fact and confirming that they had done everything possible to improve their relationships, most of these clients immediately filed the divorce paperwork. And for almost all of these folks, letting go of the unhealthy relationship was the best decision they'd ever made. Rather than becoming harder, life actually got much easier, because they no longer had the added burden of taking care of the people who were supposed to be their partners or dealing with the many negative emotions their spouses elicited from them. What they had feared prior to taking action never manifested. They realized that they had postponed their own fulfillment and happiness for months, sometimes years.

■ *Case Example:* Barry and Penny's Story

Barry was at wit's end with his wife Penny, who constantly lamented being in physical or emotional pain. It seemed that she always played the victim. Barry felt that he always had to protect her and take care of her.

He didn't want this role anymore. He wanted to be with someone who was more his equal. He was ready to walk, when his best friend suggested couples therapy, something he had previously been opposed to. He only agreed to counseling so that he could look back and say that he'd done all he could. Penny was more than happy to attend counseling with him.

In the first session, I learned that Penny came from a long line of alcoholics. I referred her to a 12-step program to work on her issues from being the adult child of an alcoholic, and continued seeing them as a couple.

Although it took some time, Penny got stronger, which shifted the dynamic between her and Barry. Penny began taking charge of her own life and stopped looking to her husband to save her or do for her what she could do for herself. For the first time ever in their relationship, they were partners.

Barry fell in love with his wife all over again, and they went on to enjoy a very fulfilling marriage. Barry's last-ditch effort had worked, primarily because of his and Penny's willingness to give it a shot and improve their dynamic. This couple had been on the brink of divorce, but Barry saw that he honestly hadn't given Penny the opportunity to respond to his needs. Assuming that it was hopeless, he had been ready to leave his wife.

What differentiates Kelly's situation from Barry and Penny's is that Kelly's primary concern was that her husband would fall apart and her kids would suffer. She disregarded her own suffering as if it didn't matter, or certainly as if it mattered less than her husband's and children's suffering. Barry had become so tired of taking care of his wife's needs that the pendulum swung in the opposite direction to the point where he didn't consider Penny at all in his decision. Kelly had to add more of her needs into the mix, while Barry had to diminish his needs to find balance.

Another important distinction between these two situations is that Kelly had tried to work with her husband on the marriage, but he had refused to work with her. He had no desire or willingness to put in the work that the marriage clearly required. He was sapping Kelly's life force with no end in sight.

On the other hand, Penny and Barry were caught in a dynamic in which she drained his life force; however, she was more than willing to work on the relationship dynamic. As a result, they were able to change the previous unhealthy pattern to a much more workable and equal partnership.

The Workability Factors

There are certain factors that suggest a relationship is workable and salvageable. There are other factors in marriages that, if present, indicate a low probability that the relationship will ever be healthy or fulfilling. I call these the *workability factors*.

As mentioned earlier in the book, if both parties are willing to put in the work that the marriage requires, the chances of the problems and issues being resolved increase dramatically. However, even when both spouses want the marriage to last, there are some situations that lack enough of the necessary ingredients to keep it afloat.

In chapter 5, I introduced the marital hierarchy of needs, consisting of five levels of needs: survival, safety, love, esteem, and actualization. The workability factors are really only pertinent to the three middle-level needs—safety, love, and esteem needs—because if a marriage has descended to survival mode, it is, by definition, not a workable situation. On the other hand, if a marriage operates at the actualization level, it is a highly functioning marriage, whose lower-level needs are met.

The following figures further outline these needs to demonstrate what must be present for the marriage to work. Each chart describes workable and unworkable scenarios in a marriage, as well as what intervention would be needed to transform an unworkable situation into one that can work.

FIGURE 7: SAFETY NEEDS

Workable If Present	Unworkable If Present	Workable with Intervention* If Both Spouses Are Willing to Work on Issues
Mutual trust	Lack of trust	Broken but reparable trust
Honesty	Pathological dishonesty	Honesty
Sense of safety (mental, emotional, physical, and financial)	Lack of safety (mental, emotional, physical, and financial)	Mutual desire to create a safe environment (mental, emotional, physical, and financial)
Good communication	No communication	Some communication
Care and concern for each other	Lack of care or concern for each other	Care and concern for each other
Kindness (no abuse)	Extreme abuse (physical, sexual, emotional, verbal, or mental)	Moderate levels of emotional, mental, or verbal abuse** (physical and sexual abuse are considered extreme abuse and will not likely change without long-term interventions)

* Intervention can take the form of therapy; mediation; support from clergy, a friend, or relative; or even just the two of you sitting down and discussing the issues and coming up with ground rules.

** This is true unless one or both of you have a no-tolerance policy.

FIGURE 8: LOVE NEEDS

Workable If Present	Unworkable If Present	Workable with Intervention* If Both Spouses Are Willing to Work on Issues
Mutual love	Absence of mutual love	Foundation of mutual love
Fidelity	Infidelity	Infidelity
Shared interests	No shared interests	Some shared interests
Commitment to the marriage from both spouses	One or both are not fully committed to the marriage	One or both are unsure of their commitment to the marriage
Reciprocal partnership	One-sided relationship	More reciprocal than one-sided

* Intervention can take the form of therapy; mediation; support from clergy, a friend, or relative; or even just the two of you sitting down and discussing the issues and coming up with ground rules.

FIGURE 9: ESTEEM NEEDS

Workable If Present	Unworkable If Present	Workable with Intervention* If Both Spouses Are Willing to Work on Issues
Self-esteem and esteem from spouse	No esteem from self or spouse and no desire to change	Low self-esteem or esteem from spouse
Mutual respect	No respect at all	A foundation of respect
Common goals	No common goals	Some common goals
Willingness of both spouses to work on marriage	Unwillingness of at least one spouse to work on marriage	Resistance from at least one spouse to work on marriage

* Intervention can take the form of therapy; mediation; support from clergy, a friend, or relative; or even just the two of you sitting down and discussing the issues and coming up with ground rules.

A Word About Betrayals

Sometimes there are betrayals or ruptures in the marriage that you and your spouse are trying to heal. If that is the case, you can see from figure 10 that as long as both parties are willing to work on getting on the other side of the breach, the marriage can often be salvaged.

FIGURE 10: BETRAYALS

Workable If Present	Unworkable If Present	Workable with Intervention* If Both Spouses Are Willing to Work on Issues
One affair with remorse	One or more affairs without remorse	Multiple affairs with remorse and willingness to seek professional help (e.g., therapy)
Addiction with awareness and/or recovery	Addiction with denial	Addiction with some awareness and willingness to get and stay clean/sober/abstinent
Financial deception with remorse	Financial deception without remorse	Financial deception with remorse (e.g., willingness to pay restitution to spouse or somehow make up for loss)
Episodes of emotional, mental, or verbal abuse with remorse	Episodes of emotional, mental, or verbal abuse without remorse	Episodes of emotional, mental, or verbal abuse with remorse and willingness to seek professional help when needed (e.g., anger management)

* Intervention can take the form of therapy; mediation; support from clergy, a friend, or relative; or even just the two of you sitting down and discussing the issues and coming up with ground rules.

There may be many other types of situations that have occurred in your marriage that you can apply the same principles to.

This exercise asks you to evaluate which workability factors are present and which are lacking. On a scale of 1 to 10, circle the number that you believe best describes the workability factors currently present in your marriage.

1. Trust

   1　　2　　3　　4　　5　　6　　7　　8　　9　　10

   lack of trust　　　　　　　　　　　　　　　mutual trust

2. Honesty

   1　　2　　3　　4　　5　　6　　7　　8　　9　　10

   pathological dishonesty　　　　　　　　　　　honesty

3. Safety

   1　　2　　3　　4　　5　　6　　7　　8　　9　　10

   lack of safety　　　　　　　　　　　　　　　safety

4. Communication

   1　　2　　3　　4　　5　　6　　7　　8　　9　　10

   no communication　　　　　　　　good communication

5. Concern for each other

   1　　2　　3　　4　　5　　6　　7　　8　　9　　10

   no concern for other　　　　　care and concern for other

6. Kindness

   1　　2　　3　　4　　5　　6　　7　　8　　9　　10

   extreme abuse　　　　　　　　　kindness (no abuse)

7. Love

   1　　2　　3　　4　　5　　6　　7　　8　　9　　10

   lack of mutual love　　　　　　　　　　　mutual love

8. Fidelity

   1　　2　　3　　4　　5　　6　　7　　8　　9　　10

   infidelity　　　　　　　　　　　　　　　　fidelity

9. Shared interests

    1   2   3   4   5   6   7   8   9   10

no shared interests   shared interests

10. Commitment

    1   2   3   4   5   6   7   8   9   10

one or both not committed   both spouses committed

11. Partnership

    1   2   3   4   5   6   7   8   9   10

one-sided relationship   reciprocal partnership

12. Esteem (from self and spouse)

    1   2   3   4   5   6   7   8   9   10

no esteem from self   high esteem from self

or spouse   and spouse

13. Respect

    1   2   3   4   5   6   7   8   9   10

no respect   mutual respect

14. Common goals

    1   2   3   4   5   6   7   8   9   10

no common goals   common goals

15. Willingness to work on marriage

    1   2   3   4   5   6   7   8   9   10

unwillingness to   willingness to

work on marriage   work on marriage

Addiction Assessment: Because addiction is a category unto itself, following are additional questions to help you discern whether the addiction in question is a workable issue in your marriage. These questions refer to any type of addiction you or your spouse may have. This includes addictions to drugs, alcohol, sex, shopping, gambling, and workaholism, among many others, as well as eating disorders. Behaviors that qualify as addictions are compulsions (repeatedly taking an action without thinking through the consequences), obsessions (something that consumes one's thoughts), or physical dependence (when physical symptoms are present as a result of withdrawal; for example, hangover, agitation, or malaise).

1. Is there an addiction present with either or both of you?
   Me: Yes ☐ No ☐ Not sure ☐
   My spouse: Yes ☐ No ☐ Not sure ☐

2. If so, is there a willingness to get into recovery?
   Me: Yes ☐ No ☐ Not sure ☐
   My spouse: Yes ☐ No ☐ Not sure ☐

3. Is the co-addict willing to get support?
   Me: Yes ☐ No ☐ Not sure ☐
   My spouse: Yes ☐ No ☐ Not sure ☐

4. Is there anything else about the addiction that you feel is important to acknowledge here?
   Describe: _____

Addiction can sometimes be hard to define and can be seriously problematic to a marriage and a family, I recommend seeking professional support or guidance from a recovery program such as the 12-step programs or other recovery-oriented resources.

The good news about addiction is that if there is a sincere desire on the part of the addict and the co-addict to get some professional help or join a recovery program, the prognosis is excellent for developing a healthier relationship.

Affirming Your Truth

In the previous section, you learned the top three considerations for knowing whether you should stay or go. To review, they are:

1. Are you moving toward a goal or away from pain?

2. Are you balancing your needs with those of your children and spouse?

3. Is your situation workable? (For example, is your spouse willing to be honest and work on the marriage with you to create a workable and agreeable relationship?)

You have just completed perhaps the toughest set of exercises in this book. Take a minute to breathe, let your answers sink in, and if you care to, in your journal write any feelings that have come up for you as a result of examining yourself and your marriage so closely. What did you learn about yourself, your spouse, or your marriage?

Knowing *Why* You Should Stay or Go

The most common reasons why people stay in their marriages are usually quite understandable. However, at the same time, I've seen many people use these reasons as excuses for remaining in unhealthy situations. I often refer to them as "misguided reasons" for staying in a bad marriage. They include (in order of how often they are used) the kids, money and security, love (this is misguided, because a marriage requires much more than love to be workable), fear, guilt, comfort and familiarity, pain avoidance, maintaining friendships and relationships with relatives (such as in-laws), keeping up appearances, and keeping promises.

When you have a tolerable marriage, staying for the kids can help them, but if you and your spouse constantly fight or have a great deal of contention between you, staying together will probably harm your children. It's important to consider what you model for your children about marriage and relationships, and ask yourself if you are conveying good messages about marriage.

If security is important to you and you are not terribly unhappy, the marriage may be good enough for you. Some would judge this as wrong and deem it a superficial reason for staying, but the premise of marriage has been based on security (financial and otherwise) for centuries. This is a personal decision that only you can make. If you are staying for the security but are unhappy or enduring abuse in some way, I suggest working on developing your financial independence. For example, if you have been out of the workforce for some time raising your kids, begin rekindling old contacts, get back into school, or take a job that could be a stepping-stone to where you want to ultimately land.

If you feel fearful or guilty about leaving but are in a highly unworkable marriage, I suggest that you get some type of counseling or support. Both of these emotions are healthy, but allowing them to factor into your choices will probably not yield the best decisions.

As with security, some people feel that staying for comfort, to avoid pain, and to keep up appearances are reasons enough to remain married. If you are reasonably happy, there's nothing wrong with choosing to stay. But if your needs aren't being met, you will likely end up hurting yourself or your spouse in some way (physically, mentally, or emotionally) by staying.

Staying married when you are unhappy just to maintain friendships and relationships with in-laws or other family members is understandable but can be quite damaging to you and others. While these outside relationships can be beneficial for a variety of reasons, I encourage you to think long and hard about whether this is truly *enough* reason to stay with your spouse. It's also important to keep in mind that the people with whom you have deep, meaningful relationships will remain a part of your life regardless of your marital status.

Finally comes the reason of wanting to remain married because you took a vow to stay "until death do you part." This is an honorable desire, and many people believe that you stay *no matter what*. However, if you are truly unhappy or living in an unhealthy situation, the vows have already been broken. Part of what the marriage vows address is *taking care* of each other. If you and your spouse don't care for each other reciprocally, you may have more of a legal arrangement than a marriage.

These misconceptions keep couples in unfulfilling or unhappy marriages, and are based on what I consider to be impure reasoning. But what is a *good* reason to stay or go? This is actually subjective territory, but I will attempt to clarify the differences. As you can see, every one of these misguided reasons can also be a perfectly valid reason to stay. This is where the motive piece comes in.

So much depends on the level of thinking the motive comes from. Generally, *moving toward a goal* is a higher level of thinking than *moving away from something you want to avoid*. For example, working toward a college degree comes from a more advanced and mature place than wanting to avoid being poor or homeless. Your motive is to be empowered rather than to avoid disempowerment.

Because I'm aware of the potential for misinterpretation and abuse of this concept, I will elaborate. Someone might say, "I wanted to feel happier, so I left my husband. I was going *toward empowerment and happiness* and *away from disempowerment and unhappiness*," without any real attempt to work on the relationship. Certainly, that action may be necessary, but marriage is a commitment to be taken seriously. By virtue of our throwaway mentality, many people today see marriage as "just another relationship," "a financial arrangement," or simply "not that big a deal." They view divorce in the same way. That's why there are social and political groups vehemently trying to reinforce the importance of commitment. It's important that you be as honest as possible about your motives to stay or leave your marriage.

Exercise: Uncovering Your Motives

The preceding section focused heavily on the motivation behind your decision-making process, not just surface reasons for staying in or leaving your marriage. In answering the following questions, see if you can gain some clarity on the motivation behind your reasoning.

A. At the moment, do you feel more inclined to stay in your marriage or leave it?

   1. If you feel more inclined to stay, why do you believe this is a better decision?

   2. What would be your *motive* for staying? (For instance, "I don't want people to think badly of me" or "I want to see how well therapy will help our situation.")

   3. If you feel more inclined to leave, why do you believe that this is the better decision?

   4. What would your *motive* be for leaving? (For instance, "I am tired of taking care of others" or "I have mentally and emotionally outgrown my spouse.")

B. What *goal* would your decision move you toward? (For instance, "I will be more independent" or "I will grow as a partner.")

C. What *goal* would your decision move you away from? (For instance, "I will get away from an oppressive environment" or "I will not be alone.")

D. In your honest appraisal, do you believe you want to stay in your marriage to move *toward a goal*, such as a deeper relationship, or *to avoid a fear* or a consequence? Write more about this in your journal.

E. In your journal write about what, if any, insights you gained from answering these questions. Did you notice any shift in your inclination? Do you feel more or less certain what to do next?

If you are more certain which way to go, you may feel somewhat relieved. If you are clear that you want to stay in your marriage, you can skip the rest of this chapter and chapters 7 and 8, and go right to chapter 9.

If you are clear that you want to leave your spouse or are still unclear about the next step, continue reading.

Are You Looking for the Easy Way Out?

Only you know whether or not you have put your heart and soul into your marriage. Only you know how happy or unhappy you are. Only you know if you're trying to get instant gratification or avoid dealing with some challenges.

In Ron and Cheryl's story in chapter 3, you saw the example of Ron, who was initially more inclined to leave his marriage than be honest with his wife about his feelings and needs. Unfortunately, this is not as uncommon as we would like to believe. Some people would rather cut ties with their spouses and move to the next relationship than look honestly at themselves.

After examining your own reasons for wanting to leave, if you feel that your desire to leave is based on a true need or something you can never change (you have tried over and over again to no avail), then your motive to leave is probably less about avoiding the problem and more about moving toward taking care of your own mental health.

By no means is divorce easy, but it can seem justified to people who don't want to look at their own inner demons or ask their spouses for what they need, or who would rather complain about others.

Exercise: Have You Really Worked Hard Enough?

This is the only section that asks you to dig as deep as you can and then a little more to uncover whether any part of you is considering divorce because it seems easier than working on yourself or your marriage, or it seems like the quicker route to feeling better. It's the fine-tooth comb portion of examining your reasoning and motives for staying married or divorcing.

A. This exercise is not meant to elicit judgment from you or anyone else but is instead designed with the hope of preventing you from looking back on your decision to leave with such regrets as, "I really didn't think it through well enough" or "I took the easy way out and wish I had given my marriage more of a chance."

1. List all that you have done to face the issues in your marriage (including reading this book). Do you truly feel that you have done all that you could? Why or why not?

2. Is there a part of you that feels you might be trying to take the "easy way out"? Why or why not?

3. How have you maintained a sense of integrity in working on your marriage? (For example, you stopped a behavior your spouse had warned would be a deal breaker if you continued, you were honest with your spouse, or you took initiative to get the relationship back on track.)

4. How have you lost a sense of integrity in working (or not working) on your marriage? (For example, you didn't do your part to maintain good communication with your spouse, you led a double life, or you gave up.)

B. Ask a trusted friend, clergyperson, doctor, or therapist to look at your list and give you honest feedback, as well as ideas for what other techniques or tactics you might try to preserve your marriage.

Does Your Spouse Qualify as a Friend?

Sharing in a Contemplating Divorce group one day, Tina realized that her husband didn't even make the grade as a friend. Noticeably pained by this awareness, she revealed, "He's not kind to me, he has no respect for me, we don't do anything together, and sometimes I wonder whether he would even notice if I never came home again!" Tina added that if this were a girlfriend, she would feel quite justified in dumping her without hesitation.

Then why would she accept this treatment from her spouse, who was supposed to be held to an even higher standard than a friend? When asked this, Tina responded that she didn't want to hurt the kids, was afraid of losing money, wanted to avoid conflict, and didn't want to be single; and this situation was just what she knew. You may recognize many of the reasons that we poked holes in earlier, because they are about avoiding something feared rather than moving toward a goal.

Tina was busted and knew it. No one in the group judged her. In fact, almost all of the other women could relate closely. Rather than get defensive, Tina just sank into her chair, sipped her tea, made a commitment to the group that she would ask her husband to treat her better, and added that she would commit to treating him more like a friend as well. Although she expressed a lack of hope that he would respond positively, she felt that taking these steps would satisfy her need to feel as if she'd done everything reasonably possible to save the marriage.

Exercise: Comparing Marriage to Friendship

This exercise asks you to compare the way you treat your spouse to the way you treat friends.

A. Next to each activity listed, answer yes if your friendships enjoy these activities and no if they don't. Do the same to assess your marriage. There are spaces at the bottom of the chart for adding your own statements of what is important to you.)

Activity	Friends		Spouse	
We talk openly, honestly, and often.	Y	N	Y	N
We're sincerely interested in each other's lives.	Y	N	Y	N
We want to spend time together.	Y	N	Y	N
We lean on each other for support.	Y	N	Y	N
We get through disagreements in a healthy way.	Y	N	Y	N
We have fun together.	Y	N	Y	N
We are considerate of each other.	Y	N	Y	N

B. How does your marriage compare to your friendships? Journal about your findings.

An even lower standard of interaction than spouses or friends is that of roommates. Whenever unhappy couples resign themselves to merely cohabitating, it is not unlike a roommate situation: there is no love between the spouses, there are no shared interests, and their lives don't intersect in any area except perhaps co-parenting (and when the relationship is very strained, there is not even co-parenting). Staying together is an arrangement, not a marriage.

But, as you know, there is a lot more to marriage than living in the same home, raising children together, and wearing a wedding band.

A. This exercise helps you evaluate how compatible and happy you are with your spouse. In the first column of the space below, place a check mark next to all the traits you would want in an ideal roommate.

Trait	Ideal Roommate Is/Has	Spouse Is/Has
Very clean/neat	☐	☐
Sloppy	☐	☐
Likes to cook	☐	☐
Likes kids	☐	☐
Good with money	☐	☐
Bad with money	☐	☐
Respectful	☐	☐
Generous	☐	☐
Works hard	☐	☐
Likes movies	☐	☐
Very social	☐	☐
A loner	☐	☐

Drinks socially	☐	☐
Doesn't drink	☐	☐
Does drugs	☐	☐
In recovery	☐	☐
Good humor	☐	☐
Serious	☐	☐
Watches lots of TV	☐	☐
Loves the outdoors	☐	☐
Other (add more traits)		
_____	☐	☐
_____	☐	☐

B. Using the same list as above, in the second column check off which traits your spouse possesses.

C. Compare the lists. How does your spouse measure up as a friend or a roommate? If this were a friend or roommate, and not the person you married, would you end the friendship or tell him or her that you no longer want to live together? In your journal write any feelings that emerged from doing this exercise.

As a result of these exercises, you may realize that your spouse does possess and demonstrate the right qualities, and you may have become clearer with the idea of staying and continuing to work on your marriage. You may have received validation that there is enough good in your marriage to work with.

On the other hand, if your spouse doesn't measure up as a friend or roommate, you may realize that he or she is not much of a partner and that you don't want to remain married. Seeing how and where your spouse falls short can be a lot to absorb. It may take you a while to integrate this information and take action. While it can be scary, putting an end to enduring unacceptable behavior from your spouse can be a very healing turn of events.

Knowing *When* You Should Stay or Go

Most people caught in the marital indecision cycle actually know what they need to do but worry about staying too long or leaving too soon. If they stay too long, they may fear being too old to date again, enjoy life more fully, move to a new area, or model healthier relationships for their children. Leaving too soon can make you doubt that you hung in there long enough or can bring pain from not seeing something through to the end, as well as later regrets for not having been or done enough while married.

Such second-guessing is a function of being human and needing to control how life turns out. I can't emphasize enough that there is not necessarily right timing, but there *is* wrong timing. The stories in the sections "Consequences of Leaving When You Should Stay" and "Consequences of Staying When You Should Leave" exemplify this point.

Waiting for External Signs

Perhaps you believe that if you wait long enough, you will get some kind of sign that says what to do next. If you are leaning toward leaving your marriage, you will be on the lookout for an event that makes it clear that it's "the right time to leave." The problem is, there is no *right* time to leave. You will find that there is always something just around the corner. A major life event such as a new home, a new baby, a new job, retirement, anniversaries, birthdays, and major or even minor holidays (such as Valentine's Day, Mother's Day, and Father's Day) are enough for some to justify not taking action to improve their situations. These reasons may be warranted or, when used year after year, may be nothing more than convenient excuses to stall making a decision or taking an action.

If you are inclined to stay in your marriage, you may search for signs of improvement in your circumstances: your partner will finally hear, trust, or respect you; or you and your spouse will finally resolve the issues causing tensions between you. You may search for crumbs without realizing that you deserve the whole cake. Make sure that if you stay, you get the whole cake!

And if you are looking for external signs indicating whether to stay or leave, you will likely remain perpetually ambivalent. Because your focus is unclear, your vision will remain blurred.

You Can't Always Trust Your Gut

Although you have reached the point where you are serious enough in your contemplation of divorce that you are reading this book, for most of you, there's a good chance that, on some level, you still believe that your marriage could work. I have seen this in couples with *years* of evidence to the contrary. In my experience, it is a rare person or couple who can let go without some form of questioning, wishing, or doubting that they did enough.

The people who leave their spouses often question whether it was right to leave when they did. I also know many people who stayed in their marriages far longer than, in hindsight, they wish they had because they didn't *feel* ready to leave. In both circumstances, these people thought it should feel right, that there should be some kind of inner knowing. They kept waiting for it to seem right, for their instincts to kick in, or for that still, small voice to direct them, but instead there were always two voices: one that justified staying and the other leaving.

When grappling with such a big decision as whether or not to stay married, you may have to take action even when there is more than one voice in your heart telling you what to do. When you know and expect this, you can contain the confusion and move ahead.

The good news is that you don't have to decide everything all at once. You can take small steps in one direction or the other, see if it feels right, and then decide what is next. For example, many people considering divorce first move into separate bedrooms to get space from their spouses. If that feels right, the next step may be for one spouse to take an extended trip or leave the house to stay with a friend, and see what that experience is like.

It's important to take a baby step, notice how it feels and what happens, take another baby step, and again see what happens and how you feel. This is true regardless of whether you are moving toward or away from each other.

It may sound funny, but this works even for those who are recommitting to their marriages. For example, when trust has been breached, it can be tricky to rebuild it. My client Karina illustrates this dynamic. When she discovered that her husband, Gus, had cheated on her, he expressed regret and decided to recommit to her. From Karina's perspective, it sounded great, but she couldn't get inside Gus's head to know whether he sincerely felt these feelings. It took her a while to regain confidence and see that his actions did indeed match his words.

■ *Case Example:* Gloria's Story

When Gloria called me in 2001, she was investigating what life might be like if she left her husband of twenty-seven years. As a result of speaking with me, family-law attorneys, and people who had already divorced or were in the process, she gathered a great deal of information on the topic, such as the legal, financial, and emotional aspects; how to tell the kids; whether she should move; and much more. After becoming more informed, she decided that she still wasn't quite ready to take this leap. Her husband had just changed jobs, his mother was dying, and the kids would leave home soon enough. She felt that the timing wasn't quite right.

Three years later, she called to tell me that her husband had just changed jobs again, his mother (who had been given six months to live the first time around) was still alive, and her kids, who hadn't left home yet, were helping make her life more miserable. She finally got that, unless she made some different choices, the people in her life would never change of their own volition.

Gloria decided that, since her husband wouldn't move out, she would. As soon as she found an acceptable apartment, she left her husband and grown children behind.

At first she felt peace and quiet but within two weeks was tormented with serious doubts about following through with the divorce. She kicked herself for having stayed and then again for leaving.

The moral of the story is that there is not always a clear internal sign. Stop waiting for it. There is rarely a definitive internal answer one way or another, so stop expecting the ambivalence to go away.

You will probably learn more in hindsight than foresight. I encourage you to do the best you can with the information you have, be thoughtful of others, try to learn from others' experiences, and maintain a sense of integrity with yourself and your loved ones.

Because you are probably still with your spouse, you don't need to know when to stay. However, you do need to get a clearer sense of when to leave, if you do leave.

For this exercise, you will need three calendars: the current year's, last year's, and next year's.

A. Start by looking at last year's calendar. View the entire year and see if you can identify times during the year when you could have left your spouse. These could be pockets of inactivity or particularly bad spells in your relationship. Hindsight is 20/20, so now it may be easy to see when you could have left your spouse. Write about those times, answering the following questions:

   1. What was going on in your marriage that made you want to leave?

   2. What prevented you from leaving?

   3. Looking back, does that reason still seem valid? Why or why not?

B. Now look at this year's calendar. See if you can identify times in the recent past or near future that might be better times to leave than others. What is the likelihood that you will make a move to separate?

   1. What is going on in your marriage that makes you want to leave?

   2. What prevents you from leaving?

   3. Does that reason seem valid? Why or why not?

   4. Are there similarities between the answers for section A and the answers you just gave?

   5. How do you feel about that?

C. Sometimes it's easier to schedule a major life change farther in the future. In examining next year's calendar, see how it feels to identify a "must leave by" date. Then, see what thoughts or emotions come up for you as you write a plan to leave.

D. What have you just learned about yourself, your situation, your resistance, your goals, and your motives?

The next subsection will help you learn the potential consequences of making the wrong move at the wrong time. Often there is some type of indication from you, your spouse, or your children that a misstep has taken place. Sometimes these wrong moves can be corrected, and as you will see, sometimes they can't.

While you can't always predict others' reactions, this subsection will highlight for you the importance of carefully thinking through the timing of your decision to the best of your ability.

Consequences of Leaving When You Should Stay

You're not happy. You want out of your pain. You think you want to leave your spouse but keep getting indications that it's not the right time. Distinguishing between what your head tells you and what your heart says isn't easy at this point. Sometimes when people think they want out badly enough, they leave impulsively with a "let the chips fall where they may" attitude. It is not so much the fact that they wanted separation from their spouses, or even that they left, but the lack of consideration of their spouses' and children's needs that causes tremendous fallout.

Let's look at some cases where people clearly left at the wrong time. Each story outlines two lessons that each couple learned as a result of their experience, so that you can learn from them.

■ *Case Example:* Doug and Miranda's Story

On the eve of his son's tenth birthday, Doug felt ready to explode. With the family pressure off the charts, the tension in the house was just too much for him. He didn't have the energy to care about his son's important event and the family obligations; he didn't care about the family trip scheduled for the following week; he didn't care that his and Miranda's anniversary was a month and a half away. He had let his emotional upset reach a point where things were coming to a head, and he feared a potential nervous breakdown.

As Doug saw it, he only had two choices: (1) have a major blowout with Miranda once and for all or (2) leave. He chose the second option, thinking it would create the least amount of waves. Though his departure was quieter than a shouting match would have been, the impact was tremendous nonetheless.

Doug's son Cody awoke on his birthday looking forward to the family's celebrating with him, but Miranda had to tell him that his dad was gone. Cody was devastated, thinking that his dad left because he had done something wrong. Instead of the best day of his young life, this birthday was, by far, the worst.

When Doug later learned of his departure's impact on Cody, he felt terrible. He realized that he should have thought more about preparing his family for his leaving, and perhaps even waited a week later to take off.

Lessons Learned

1. Prepare your family as best you can mentally, emotionally, and financially for the separation.

2. Avoid leaving during important holidays or celebrations.

■ *Case Example:* Gillian and Dennis's Story

Although on some level, Gillian felt tremendous relief, even two years after leaving her six-year marriage with Dennis, she also felt that she had been shortsighted, and was plagued by guilt and remorse. She felt that she could have, and should have, done more to save the marriage. At the time of their separation, however, she just wanted out. She couldn't imagine spending another day married to Dennis.

At one point, Gillian thought about asking Dennis if she could move back in, but when she hinted at the idea, Dennis let her know that he had moved on and that reuniting wasn't an option.

Every waking moment (and even many sleeping moments) for Gillian was filled with some version of beating herself up for leaving, for not following through on the assignments their therapist had given them, for having taken what she felt had been the easy way out, and on and on.

Being free from her marriage didn't bring her the peace she had thought it would. Her negative self-talk could not let her enjoy that she had followed her own truth, knowing that the marriage had been killing a part of her. In retrospect, she thought she could have done more to work on things, and mercilessly blamed herself for throwing away the marriage.

In hindsight, Gillian felt that she should have done more research by reading and talking to others with similar circumstances to fully understand all the repercussions such an impulsive departure might cause. It wasn't until after "jumping" that she began seeking more information on what divorce was really all about.

Lessons Learned

1. Do everything in your power to make your marriage work.

2. View this major life decision from a big-picture perspective as well as from the "here and now" viewpoint by doing as much advance research as possible.

■ *Case Example:* Bill and Sally's Story

After a great deal of mutual fighting and abuse, Bill decided to move out of the house. Rather than seek professional guidance, read books, or get any kind of support, Bill and Sally forged ahead with their divorce.

Their daughter, Megan, was at the pinnacle of her gymnastics career at age fourteen. She was in junior Olympic competitions winning medals left and right. Her world revolved around her meets, and she was even homeschooled so that she could travel all over the world to compete. There was no question that Megan was an exceptional athlete who was headed for greatness.

Bill and Sally didn't consider enough how their split might impact Megan's future career. With two households to support, they could no longer afford Megan's coach, her gymnastics program, or the travel expenses for her competitions.

Megan's life and destiny were changed forever. On the one hand, although Megan missed seeing her father every day, she was somewhat relieved when her parents split up, because she didn't like feeling the tension and disdain between them. But in losing her life's *focus and purpose, she became clinically depressed. Megan's coach had been like a second mother, so Megan mourned the loss of that relationship tremendously.*

Six months later, when Megan's maternal grandmother found out what had happened, she offered some financial assistance, but it was too late. The program Megan would've joined had already started, and by the next opportunity to participate, she would have been too old to qualify.

If Bill and Sally had created some type of financial plan; researched scholarships (which they also later found out existed); or even sought assistance from friends, family, or divorce professionals, this level of impact on Megan might have been averted.

Lessons Learned

1. In as many of these areas as you can—financially, emotionally, mentally, and physically—ask for support and guidance before taking action.

2. Consider how your children's lives will be impacted, and wherever possible, maintain their schools, programs, and support networks.

Consequences of Staying When You Should Leave

I know it's hard to leave. I know that there will be lots of change and upheaval. I know that it may mean getting completely out of your comfort zone and perhaps risking quite a lot. But *staying* in your unhappy or unhealthy marriage in an attempt to avoid pain and discomfort, when you know in your heart you should leave, may actually bring more pain and discomfort into your life.

Struggling to keep a sinking relationship afloat takes effort. There are thousands of people who are totally unaware of how much energy is sapped from them as they continue trying to make a bad situation good.

In a recent Contemplating Divorce workshop I held, one woman said that it wasn't until she looked at years of family photos that she realized how unhappy she was. Her photos showed her transformation from a happy, vibrant, confident woman to a sad, beaten down, tired-looking woman. It was what had happened to her mother, and she had sworn that she would not let it happen to her. This realization was the impetus she needed to take action.

This subsection focuses primarily on case studies of people who suffered from staying when it was clearly the right time to leave their bad marriages.

■ *Case Example:* Joyce and Brian's Story

Joyce's husband, Brian, had engaged in multiple affairs, which she didn't like but had put up with for several years. She had ended their sexual relationship four years earlier, after the birth of their third child. Things were not that unhappy between them, other than having a sexless marriage. Joyce felt that, since she wasn't interested in having sex with him again and he was just sleeping with women here and there, she could simply look the other way and no one would get hurt.

But then something happened that absolutely devastated her: Brian not only started sleeping with her best friend, Luanne, but they fell in love, and Brian now wanted to divorce Joyce so he could marry Luanne. Joyce felt incredibly betrayed by both Brian and Luanne, especially since Luanne had been her confidant and knew what she had been through in her marriage.

Brian admitted later that he was tired of pretending that things were okay. He said he purposely took an extreme action to "push the envelope" and cause the divorce to happen, because he had felt as if Joyce were holding him hostage. While he hadn't actually intended to fall in love with Luanne, he knew that once Joyce discovered that they had slept together, she would probably kick him out, which would free him from the trap.

Lessons Learned

1. Pretending that a problem does not exist, in an effort to avoid it, is merely a form of denial. The problem still exists, and you need to deal with it.

2. Failure to deal with a problem in a timely manner will cause the problem to grow; you will be better off if you deal with problems when they arise.

■ *Case Example:* Barbara and Curt's Story

Barbara and Curt had been separated for three years, partly because they were unhappy together and partly because Curt got a new job seven hundred miles away. Having previously been unemployed for over a year, he couldn't pass up this opportunity.

Barbara gave him her blessings but let him know that she would not leave the home she adored and the life she had created just to be with him when they weren't that happy anyway. She had been through the wringer with his alcoholism and, after four costly DUIs, had had enough.

This new arrangement suited both of them, as well as their college-age children. Rather than file for divorce and deal with all the red tape, Barbara had decided to just let things be. It seemed that they had the best of both worlds; that is, until Curt lost his job because of his drinking.

They now couldn't make ends meet on Barbara's income, and since Curt couldn't find another job in a timely manner, they ended up having to sell the home that Barbara loved.

Lessons Learned

1. By not taking action to move forward, you may wind up moving backward.

2. By living apart but remaining legally attached, you may open yourself up to being impacted by your spouse's unwise choices.

■ *Case Example:* Nate and Georgia's Story

I received a call from a school counselor asking whether I could meet with a family she felt might be in some type of crisis. She wasn't sure exactly what were the dynamics but suspected that the parents were unhappily married.

The minute these parents, Nate and Georgia, and their two children, Philip and Beth, came in, I could feel the tension among them. It was extremely uncomfortable.

Beth, the youngest child, was getting in trouble at school for teasing and bullying some of the other children. Initially Beth couldn't say what was causing this, but after several sessions I uncovered some of what was going on.

Beth's mother, Georgia, had an anger management problem, and everyone in the house walked on eggshells to try to avoid making her mad. Whenever Georgia's temper flared, nine times out of ten, she took it out on her husband. She had become extremely resentful of Nate for not being a better provider and not doing his part to maintain the house and family. In many ways, he was an added burden for her. She had wanted to leave the marriage for years but, like many people, felt she needed to stay for the children.

Despite Georgia's attempts to get the message through to Nate that she needed him to help more around the house, he ignored her. It seemed that the only way she could get his attention was to fly into a rage, and yell at and belittle him. Though it did little to change him, it made her feel better for the moment.

A typical day in their house consisted of Georgia yelling at Nate (often in front of the children), and Nate, prompted by frustration and humiliation, taking it out later on Philip. Philip, in turn, teased his younger sister unmercifully, and because Beth had no one else at home to take it out on, she then became a bully to the weaker kids at school.

You may know this dynamic better as "kick the dog syndrome." It occurs when the person with the most power in a system takes out his or her frustrations on a less powerful member, and so on down the line.

In this situation, Georgia and Nate had an unhappy marriage that wasn't getting better. They had been to counseling, and she had read books, talked to friends, and tried to get Nate to emulate one of his male friends, but nothing had worked. Instead of divorce, Georgia continued squelching her inner urgings to leave her husband, and just became more and more resentful over time.

As happens so often, the children bear the brunt of the unhappiness between the spouses by absorbing the tension, carrying the unspoken emotions, and acting out. Both children suffered on some level, but Beth now called attention to her pain by getting in trouble and alienating some of the other kids at school with her behavior. Georgia's remaining in the bad marriage was meant to prevent her children's suffering, but instead it had created more suffering.

In time, and with some encouragement from her support network, Georgia did end up filing for divorce. She felt immediate relief the moment Nate moved out. The atmosphere at home went from a 10+ on the tension scale to a 3 within a week. Philip stopped teasing Beth, who miraculously stopped being a bully at school. She actually started getting better grades and even joined the girl's basketball team. Nate was also happier, and his relationship with both children improved greatly. All around, everyone felt happier and saw life improve dramatically.

Lessons Learned

1. If you don't deal directly with your marital problems, they will get your attention in other ways.

2. The whole family suffers from a tense and stressful environment.

■ *Case Example:* Lorraine's Story

The hardest conversation I've had with anyone was with a sixty-eight-year-old woman named Lorraine, who called asking for help and resources for her impending divorce. She had been unhappily married for over forty years, thinking the whole time that "one of these days" she would file the papers. She admitted that her fear of going out on her own had kept her from filing. Instead, one day her seventy-two-year-old husband decided he wanted out.

She found herself divorcing at age sixty-eight with no job skills, no assets, and no one to care for her. Because the house she lived in had been her husband's prior to their marriage, she had a small financial interest in it but certainly not enough to sustain her. They had no children together because he had three children from a prior marriage and hadn't wanted more. What little family she had lived abroad, and she didn't have enough of a connection with them to make them a viable resource for her.

Lorraine was at a total loss of what to do. Had she known twenty years ago that this would come to pass, she definitely would have divorced then. At least she could have gone back to school, obtained some work experience, and put herself in a stronger financial position. Her options now were so much more limited at her age. It broke my heart.

Lessons Learned

1. Nothing changes if nothing changes.

2. The safer and easier road now might be the harder road later on.

Exercise: Avoid Learning Lessons the Hard Way

Addressing each of the lessons learned in the case examples above, evaluate what, if anything, you need to do differently in your decision-making process. Some of these questions may be a review from previous chapters, but this will provide you with more comprehensive information with which to make a plan.

1. List any areas you are aware of in your marriage about which you have avoided discussing or taking any action.

2. By avoiding necessary action, have you seen any of the following dynamics happen? If so, describe. If not, predict how and where these dynamics might happen.

   The problem still exists and doesn't go away.

   The problem gets worse.

   The problem gets your attention in other ways.

   By not taking action to move forward, you are moving backward.

   What you thought was the easier road has become the harder road.

3. In what areas do you feel you are currently getting enough information and support?

4. In what areas do you feel you need more support? How can you get that support?

5. In what areas do you need more information? How can you get that information?

6. Are you or your family members suffering from a tense home environment? In your journal, write why you believe this is so.

7. How would your children's lives be impacted if you divorced?

8. Have you considered what timing might work best if you left? Elaborate.

9. Describe steps you have taken or are taking to protect yourself financially in the event of a divorce.

10. Describe the ways you have considered to prepare your family in the event of a separation or divorce.

Exercise: Pros and Cons List

A. In your journal form complete sentences around the following topics:

1. What I *gain by staying* in my marriage; for example, "By staying married, I have security."

2. What I *give up by staying* in my marriage; for example, "By staying married, I give up having peace in my life."

3. What I *gain by leaving* my marriage; for example, "By leaving my marriage, I gain autonomy."

4. What I *give up by leaving* my marriage; for example, "By leaving my marriage, I won't see my kids as much."

   If it helps, give each reason you've listed a priority level of 1, 2, or 3 (with 1 having the highest priority, and 3 the lowest). Compare priority levels of each reason to see which one deserves the most focus. This can be extremely helpful in distinguishing what truly matters from the less important factors in your decision.

B. If you and your spouse are talking together about splitting up, it will be helpful if both of you complete section A and compare notes. This can be a powerful tool in understanding your spouse's viewpoint and needs.

This chapter helped you look at *if*, *why*, and *when* you should stay or go. The next two chapters provide more information on *how* to divorce to help you if you are leaning more toward leaving.

Keep in mind that, most likely, any way you turn will not necessarily feel good or seem right immediately. I just want to remind you and affirm for you that the reason this is such a difficult place to be in is that there aren't necessarily any good choices. I'm sure that if you had your way, you'd have somehow rekindled the romantic flame or done things differently so that you could remain happily married.

But given your current position, all of the choices open to you at this juncture will likely entail at least some pain for you, your spouse, and your children. Be assured that there is another side to this dilemma, and coming to terms with your decision to stay or go is the first step to getting your life back.

7

Taking Action When
It's Needed

*And the day came when the risk to remain tight in a bud was more painful than
the risk it took to blossom.*

—Anaïs Nin

Chapters 7 and 8 provide a very general overview for those who plan to move ahead with filing for a divorce. Other resources exist with much more information about specific divorce issues, such as parenting through divorce, divorce and finances, and the legalities of marital dissolution, but these chapters contain valuable basic information to start the process. I believe that even those of you who are still unsure of your next step can benefit from reading these next two chapters, since knowing what divorce is like may impact your current choices.

This chapter provides an overview of the divorce options available. It also includes tips on how to save time and money, and provides general answers to some of the frequently asked questions about logistical tasks involved in marital dissolution.

Because divorce is such a big undertaking on so many levels, I want you to have as much knowledge of the process as possible so that you will know what to expect and how to navigate the entire process. Even under the best of circumstances, ending your marriage will challenge you. The more you know, the more appropriately you will respond to these challenges. Some basic legal and emotional information is included in this chapter, but refer to the suggested reading list at the end of the book for additional books on divorce.

Standing on the Edge

I remember well the feeling of standing at the edge of the high diving board, trying to conjure up the nerve to jump off. The water seemed a thousand feet away in my ten-year-old mind's eye. No matter how long I stood there, I couldn't come up with a good reason to jump off. All I could think was, "What if I land on my stomach?" or "What if I hit my head on the diving board?" or "What if I get the wind knocked out of me and drown?"

Ultimately, I would shut off my brain, run, and jump off, hoping for the best; or someone would get in line behind me and force me to move forward.

In time, I grew more confident and less afraid when diving, but I must say (not being fond of heights), I never became completely comfortable with it. Something about leaping from such heights seemed very unnatural and death defying.

Like me on the diving board, you may have stayed in your marriage and contemplated all that could go wrong if you divorced and all the reasons you shouldn't jump. It's a healthy form of self-preservation to consider the ways in which you or others around you could get hurt. Until something forces you to jump or until you can find a logical reason to risk everything you've worked so hard for, you stand there on the edge.

The Courage to Divorce

As you perch on the precipice of what feels like a thirty-thousand-foot-high cliff, you can't imagine landing on your feet. You can't even see what you would land on, so why in the world would you willingly jump into this abyss? If you've been in an unhappy, unfulfilling, or unhealthy marriage, there is a reason to jump: to get you to a different place in your life.

■ *Case Example:* Melanie's Story

After years of pain and struggle with her depressed, uncommunicative husband, Melanie gave up. She honestly felt that she had done all she could to help her husband and herself, but since he wasn't putting any effort into the marriage, she decided to move on. Melanie said, "Why should I spend another day being miserable, given how hard I have tried? I'd like to laugh again."

Melanie had reached the point in her contemplation process where she understood two things clearly: (1) her ambivalence was never going to subside, and (2) everything she had feared divorce would bring was already her reality or wasn't based in reality at all.

Case in point: Melanie had feared the anger that would come if she divorced, but her kids and husband were already angry; she feared loneliness, but if left on a desert island, she would've been less lonely than she felt in her current situation; she feared not having enough money, but the family was already struggling financially since her husband didn't work; she feared her children would suffer from the divorce, but they begged her to get divorced. They suffered from the marriage, *because they couldn't take the constant tension and fighting.*

As she sat in my office, her entire demeanor changed the moment this revelation hit her, and the swirling inside her head stopped. Her first reaction was a big smile followed immediately by some tears. The cycle of thoughts had stopped only to unmask the emotions underneath. Once she stopped distracting herself from her feelings and allowed them to just unfold, she found herself bouncing all over the emotional map. She admitted to me later that, although some of the feelings were uncomfortable, she was happy to no longer be numb. Also, a tremendous relief came to her from simply making the decision to take her life back. It was as if she had been experiencing the world in black and white, and all of a sudden, she could see in color again.

Holding Your Nose and Jumping

When you make a firm decision to dissolve your marriage, a whole new set of information and emotions shows up. You struggled for quite a while with whether or not to remain in your marriage. That ambivalent phase of decision making was confusing, stressful, fearful, and guilt ridden. But staying stuck sheltered you from some deeper feelings, both good and bad.

Once resolved, your confusion will likely give way to an inner conviction that you are doing the right thing. With this clarity, like Melanie, you may feel a sense of relief and excitement, but at the same time, your sadness and fear may intensify. The high emotional spikes will be higher and the low dips lower than when you weren't sure which direction you were headed in.

I want to emphasize again that, as certain as you can be in a moment, you will probably never feel consistently 100 percent certain that you are doing the right thing by leaving your marriage. Because of this, doubt can easily creep back in. This is where the appropriate support will make all the difference.

You're likely to cycle through the grief progression again but on a different level. You may need to refer back to chapter 3 for the full description, but I will review the process here: it goes from the initial loss to protest, then despair, detachment, and on to reorganization.

You may stay in one phase for quite a while or find yourself in all five phases in one day. This doesn't mean that you are doing anything wrong. Grief is a very personal process, and as you move forward it is important to withhold judgment of your feelings. However your process unfolds is fine. If you truly feel that you are stuck in one stage or are, at the other extreme, all over the emotional map, I recommend seeking professional counseling. This additional support will likely be very helpful in clarifying and normalizing your experience.

Exercise: Document Your Feelings

A tool that can assist you in gaining and maintaining clarity is keeping a log of your feelings and desires to proceed, as well as the confusion and sadness that accompany separating from your spouse.

If you are like most people, some days you will feel 100 percent sure that you want to leave, some days it may be more like 60 to 70 percent, and there will likely be a smattering of days where you only feel 25 percent certain that you should part ways.

Because your emotions on the matter may change every day, I recommend keeping track of them daily by keeping a notepad next to your bed and writing the thoughts and feelings you had throughout the day. You may certainly want to write more (for example, if you have an incident in which you need to clarify your thoughts or vent), but I don't recommend writing less often than once a day, at least until you are on the other side of your indecision.

FIGURE 11: THE GRIEF PROGRESSION

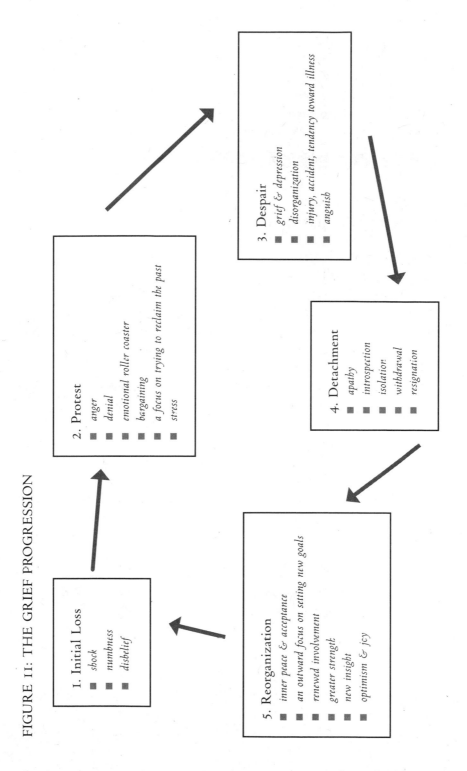

1. Initial Loss
   - shock
   - numbness
   - disbelief

2. Protest
   - anger
   - denial
   - emotional roller coaster
   - bargaining
   - a focus on trying to reclaim the past
   - stress

3. Despair
   - grief & depression
   - disorganization
   - injury, accident, tendency toward illness
   - anguish

4. Detachment
   - apathy
   - introspection
   - isolation
   - withdrawal
   - resignation

5. Reorganization
   - inner peace & acceptance
   - an outward focus on setting new goals
   - renewed involvement
   - greater strength
   - new insight
   - optimism & joy

Seeing your emotional trends in black and white may be enough to clarify the appropriate outcome for you. On days when doubt sneaks in, you can take out this documentation of your feelings and remind yourself what your truth is. Along with writing about your emotions, including specific events that occurred can be even more powerful for remembering why you don't want to stay in the marriage.

Divorce Isn't Easy, but It Is Doable

Getting a divorce is terrifying for the average person under average circumstances. You will probably feel scared throughout most of this journey, and much of the information you hear and read will seem overwhelming. As insurmountable as divorce may seem, it isn't. Thousands of people get divorced every day. The key to a better divorce is getting the support you need. One man who came in to see me jokingly asked, "What do I need, a divorce *team*?" and I answered, "Yes, you do!"

You will need friends, family, and divorce professionals to guide you and accompany you every step of the way, and there's nothing wrong with that. If you learn nothing else in your divorce process, I hope you will learn to ask for help when you need it.

I have seen people suffer needlessly and make the process much harder than necessary simply because they lacked the facts and an understanding of the divorce process. Despite the large number of marital dissolutions in this country, those facing their first divorce (and sometimes subsequent divorces as well) still feel quite lost and overwhelmed, and are not given much information on how to even begin the process. These people have no idea what to expect mentally, emotionally, or financially. They often flounder and spend much more time, money, and energy than if they had been armed with the facts and choices available to them.

Making Mistakes

Before elaborating on how best to get through your divorce, it's important to address the very natural fear of making mistakes as you go along. This information is included to help you avoid whatever errors you can foresee in your case, but you are still likely to make mistakes anyway. I urge you to be gentle with yourself when this happens.

I don't know anyone who looked back on their divorce and said that they made no mistakes. Just as in other areas of life, mistakes are an inevitable part of the process. If you become immobilized by the fear of taking a wrong turn, you will almost assuredly make the process more difficult and expensive than otherwise. You might even make more mistakes.

Those who err most are the ones who try to go it alone. Having the right divorce-support professionals, and trusting that support, can make a big difference. Not only is it okay to ask for help, it is crucial in minimizing any potential negative impact of the divorce.

When you know that mistakes are bound to happen, you will more readily trust those working with and for you, and will be more resilient when errors occur. If you feel unsure about a particular professional's advice on an issue and thus feel more likely to make a mistake, you may want to get a second opinion before moving forward, but keep in mind that this can get extremely expensive.

I've worked with many people who try to think their way through the process. It's important to think through each step, but trying to head off every little thing that can go wrong will result in paralysis. At some point, you will just have to take the next action, trusting that all will be well— maybe not as you planned or hoped, but well enough.

The next two sections provide the big-picture overview of divorce, including options for divorce proceedings, and time and money savers, followed by a focus on the smaller details with answers to frequently asked questions.

Overview of Divorce

Like so much of our world today, divorce is evolving. We're no longer bound only by the traditional litigation divorce, *War of the Roses* style. Former litigators who didn't feel good about "fighting" for their clients anymore developed alternatives to the old-school legal model of my-side-versus-your-side, where each party tries to get the most goods. While litigation still serves an important role, there are less contentious options available to divorcing couples, such as self-representation, mediation, and collaborative law. The general overview of the options includes the following.

Self-Representation (a.k.a. In Propria Persona)

In an "in pro per" case, as it's called, the person involved is self-represented, filing all the paperwork, deciphering all the legal issues, and stating his or her own case to the other side. Note: A good number of self-represented litigants consult an attorney for legal advice, but the attorney has no responsibility for representing this person and will not appear for him or her at hearings or other court proceedings.

Cost:	Low.
Time:	This mode does not necessarily cut down on the time your divorce takes. How long it takes depends more on the complexity and contentiousness of your situation.
Effectiveness:	Questionable—not usually as beneficial as hiring an attorney but can work with no or low assets, or no controversy.
Advantage:	Usually saves money; you have the greatest amount of control, because you know your situation better than an attorney.
Disadvantage:	Your lack of understanding of many of the terms or court procedures may hold up the process or make things more difficult than if you'd hired an attorney. Even if you are an attorney, you are probably too emotionally involved in the outcome to be fully effective.

Mediation

One trained mediation professional acts as a neutral party to both you and your spouse to help you come to an agreement that you both feel comfortable with on your own.

Cost:	Low, moderate, or high.
Time:	Because mediation is chosen primarily by couples who can agree on most matters, it tends to take

less time than the other divorce modalities. It is also easier to schedule meetings, given that there are usually only three people's schedules to coordinate. However, mediation can take as long as a litigated case.

Effectiveness:	Good if you both share equal knowledge (of assets, for example) and emotional power in the relationship, and if you both get along; not as good if one of you has more knowledge of money and assets, unless the one with less knowledge can be educated on all of the financial matters.
Advantage:	More times than not, you will save money. You can also have a consulting attorney as your advocate to help you think of points you might not think of on your own. You can apply your own sense of what is equitable, as opposed to following the letter of the law.
Disadvantage:	Emotional power or knowledge imbalance can affect the outcome. Mediators are not immune to being more influenced by one spouse. There's no personal advocate without additional expense.

Collaborative

This relatively new model for divorce involves two attorneys and two divorce coaches (one working with each spouse), a financial specialist, and a child specialist (both neutral professionals).

Collaborative law places less emphasis on individual spouses getting what they want, and more focus on looking at common goals. Wherever possible, shared goals are created to have something for everyone to work toward. An example of a shared goal is "wanting what's best for the kids." For instance, the parties may choose to forego 50-50 custody if it's in the children's best interest to be with one parent 70 percent of the time. The process is client centered, meaning that the agenda is driven by the spouses' wants and needs, rather than the attorneys' or court's needs or requirements.

Cost:	Moderate to high.
Time:	Cases are often resolved faster than with other modalities but can be delayed due to the difficulty of scheduling times when everyone can meet.
Effectiveness:	Good if parties have incentive or desire to cooperate; not good if serious trust or abuse issues, or serious mental illness or active addiction is present in either of you.
Advantage:	You will be assisted legally, emotionally, and financially. You have a high potential to improve your relationship with your spouse through learning new skills. You can apply your own sense of what is equitable, as opposed to following the letter of the law.
Disadvantage:	If hit with an impasse in negotiations, you both must hire new attorneys and start a different process (e.g., litigation). Expenses are higher in the beginning of the case. Scheduling can be cumbersome.

Litigation

Litigation is the most traditional style of all the legal paradigms. Each party hires his and her own attorney. Good litigators are aggressive, pursuing any and all assets they can for their clients. This modality can be quite effective but also quite expensive, and divorce proceedings can drag on for years.

While the majority of cases settle prior to trial, almost all require periodic appearances, at least by counsel, at hearings and conferences. But there is always the risk that, if a point cannot be negotiated, it will end up before a judge. If or when this happens, it is almost guaranteed that this case will cost a great deal more money, take much more time, and be much more emotionally draining on both parties.

Cases ending up in trial are often settled by a judge who knows very little about the family his or her decision impacts. In addition, with few exceptions court proceedings become matters of public record, available for anyone to view. In other words, you lose control over the outcome and your privacy in litigation.

Cost:	Moderate to extremely high.
Time:	Unpredictable, although this process is likely to last longer than the others due to the fact that settlement issues may be disputed more.
Effectiveness:	Good in resolving issues if there is an unworkable relationship between you and your spouse; not good in maintaining good relations between you and your spouse, and not usually good for children.
Advantage:	Your attorney is your advocate and represents you and your interests; ideal if you don't like or are not good at negotiating.
Disadvantage:	Can be very draining and quite costly. You have the least amount of control. Attorneys have a vested interest in not settling. You lose your privacy when the outcome becomes public record.

Exercise: Which Method Is Best for You?

1. Using this basic information about the various divorce processes, write which option you think would be best for you and why (self-representation, mediation, collaborative, or litigation).

2. Is this option realistic? Is this an option your spouse would also choose or be willing to participate in?

3. What concerns do you have?

4. What further information do you need?

5. Envision your ideal outcome in the division of assets and child custody arrangement (for example, I will have 70 percent custody and keep the house). Is this realistic?

Ideas for Saving Resources

There are three things I tell clients to do (regardless of their individual circumstances) to save time, money, and energy: do your research, learn from others, and trust your instincts.

DO YOUR RESEARCH

Do your own research to find the best help and resources for your personal situation rather than follow blindly what others have done before you. Look for local, low-fee services in the phone book or on the Internet. Read books (refer to the suggested reading list) and articles, and visit websites about divorce. Interview *several* attorneys for at least ten to fifteen minutes each (ideally, an hour) to get a sense of who would be a good fit for you. Ask each attorney about his or her area of expertise to ensure a good match.

LEARN FROM OTHERS

Learn from others by talking to various people about their divorce experiences. Ask them about their lawyers, the modalities of divorce they used, and any special circumstances that came up in their cases. Ask them what they would do differently in their divorce processes if they could turn back the clock. Involve other professionals, such as financial experts, therapists, and real estate agents. You'd be surprised how much information you can get at low or no cost from these resources.

BE IN CHARGE OF YOUR DIVORCE PROCESS

If something doesn't feel right, it probably isn't. Many people feel that they should defer to the attorney, financial planner, or accountant, because "they are the experts." However, keep in mind that all of these people are working for *you*. You have the right to ask questions, say no to their suggestions, and otherwise be in charge of your own process.

The divorce proceedings will not seem so daunting once you start gathering the facts and figures you need. You will know more, waste less, and feel more confident.

MONEY-SAVING TIP

If you have already contacted a lawyer or mediator, it's a good idea to have all of your questions written out ahead of time. The better organized your queries, the more time you will save. Keep in mind that most attorneys charge by portions of an hour (not by the actual amount of minutes you confer). For instance, if you talk to your attorney for eight minutes, you may be charged for fifteen minutes (quarter-hour increments) or twelve minutes (two-tenths of an hour). Keep track of your minutes by timing your calls and recording the time. Maximize your money spent by filling the entire time segment.

Details of Divorcing

This section answers some of the most frequently asked questions about divorcing. Answers are provided in a general enough way to apply to you no matter where you live and regardless of the details of your particular situation.

Please keep in mind that these answers do not constitute legal advice. It behooves you to get more information from experts closer to home as you go along, because divorce laws vary from state to state and sometimes county to county.

Where Do I Start?

As the first step, some of you may want to gather as much information about marital dissolution as you can before telling your spouses that you want a divorce, while some of you may prefer to inform your spouses of your desire to divorce before investigating methods and resources.

If you choose to do the research first, you run the risk that your spouse will discover that you're reading books or consulting with attorneys. This is not necessarily the wrong way to go about it, but you should be aware that your spouse's finding out accidentally can make your situation more difficult. Though it's your decision, it's worth thinking this through as best you can.

How Do I Tell My Spouse I Want a Divorce?

What, when, and how you tell your spouse will depend greatly on whether the two of you have had any previous conversations about divorce. If you've been open about your unhappiness, or know that it's mutual, your conversation will obviously be easier than if your spouse will learn about your discontent for the first time.

In a more mutual or anticipated situation, you can simply say, "I've reached a place where I'm ready to move forward with the divorce; how would you like to proceed?" or "This is how I'd like to proceed." In that case your spouse will probably respond predictably by going along with your decision or telling you what he or she needs.

However, if you've suffered in silence for years or tried to tell your spouse, only to have the information fall on deaf ears, you will receive a less predictable response from him or her. Your spouse may be stunned, angry, or extremely sad. He or she may become oppositional and threaten to take you to the cleaners and never let you see the kids again. Or your spouse may collapse emotionally. He or she may not be surprised or may express mutual feelings. The point is that you don't know what kind of reaction you'll get, which is what makes this a difficult conversation to have.

No matter what the reaction, it won't likely be a comfortable scene for either of you. Your fear of facing this type of scenario might tempt you to skip the discussion part of this process and go right to serving your spouse with the papers. Not only is this disrespectful, but this delivery will not bring the best out in anyone.

I met with a woman who was angry at her husband and wanted a divorce. She announced to me, "I'm just going to have his ass served with papers." As I told her, that's certainly one way to get the process started, but I don't recommend handling it that way. It's not going to get you the result you want in the long run.

One of the things to think about as you proceed with any step (but certainly the first step) is how your action will affect your spouse. Will it bring out the best or worst in him or her? What tone will your actions set? Dumping divorce papers in your spouse's lap will almost always incite a warfare mentality in him or her. You set the tone for the entire process when commencing on such a contentious level. While it's not impossible to back down from that position, it can be difficult, because the level of mistrust is so great from the get-go.

When you let your spouse know that you are going to the courthouse to file, and offer him or her the option to come with you, respond later, or be served, your spouse feels that he or she has some choice in the matter. Most of us react better to difficult circumstances when we feel respected and believe that our feelings have been considered.

Do I Need an Attorney?

Most people undergoing divorce think that the first step is to get an attorney. What they don't realize is that the divorce process has evolved a great deal in recent years. Because clients have so many choices today, often the best first course of action is to decide which divorce modality to utilize, then consider which (if any) attorney to employ.

Traditionally, when people began the divorce process they thought of friends and others they knew who had been divorced. They called these people and asked them for the names of their attorneys. Then, they called each attorney, met with him or her, and more times than not, hired someone without even considering that they might *not* need an attorney, at least not yet and not necessarily for all of the issues.

If you go the conventional route, you open yourself to having your chosen attorney determine the kind of divorce you will get. You run the risk of getting on the most expensive and contentious track right away.

What you should know is that anything you and your spouse can negotiate together, you don't need an attorney (or any other professional, for that matter) to negotiate for you. Most people don't even consider that this is an option. You can hire an attorney to handle just one part of your divorce, and you and your spouse can negotiate the rest. I had a couple in my practice who settled everything by themselves except for the child custody arrangement, which saved them a tremendous amount of money.

Having said this, before negotiating, I recommend hiring a consulting attorney to advise you about what offer to make. Later, when you come to your own settlement agreement with your spouse, you can hire the same or a different attorney to make sure the agreement is in your best interest and that you haven't missed an important detail.

So, it is wise to, in some capacity, consult an attorney who has your sole interest in mind, though you don't necessarily need him or her to handle every aspect of your divorce. Even in self-representation or mediation, you will usually be better off having an attorney review all documents before signing.

How Do I Find an Attorney?

Finding an attorney is easy. Finding the *right* attorney is the trick. If you look in your local yellow pages, you will see that attorneys can have many types of specializations, and there is often no shortage of them.

Asking trusted friends or neighbors whom they consulted in their divorces is a fine strategy, but most people fail to ask more questions. You will want to ask your friends what their main issues were (custody; support; asset allocation; and special circumstances such as move-away issues, addiction, and mental health problems) and how the attorney handled those issues.

You can also directly ask attorneys what they specialize in and get a sense of their personal styles. If you need a hand-holder but get someone who is gruff, your emotional needs won't likely be met, and you may wind up feeling beaten up by your lawyer in the process. If you need an aggressive lawyer but go with someone kinder and gentler, you will likely feel that your legal needs weren't met.

In addition to meeting your needs, your attorney should have a legal style that matches that of your spouse's attorney. If your spouse gets an aggressive attorney, you will need an equally aggressive one. One man I counseled was frustrated that he would have to hire a "shark," as he put it. He wanted to handle the divorce in a more amicable climate, but since his wife didn't share those sentiments, he had no choice if he wanted to be on the same par with her.

I recommend shopping around for an attorney. Call a number of different people who have been recommended to you and see who you think is the best fit for you. Make sure you feel absolutely comfortable with whomever you hire, and remember, your attorney works for you. If he or she does something that makes you feel bad or misrepresented, then you have the right to say so. If your attorney can't accommodate your needs or makes you feel bad for speaking up, then you can let this one go and find someone better suited for you. It's never ideal to have to start over with someone new and bring this new person up to speed, but the alternative of staying with an attorney who disregards your needs is a worse scenario.

As mentioned earlier in this chapter, trust your instincts: if something doesn't feel right, it probably isn't.

How Long Does It Take to Get a Divorce?

How long your divorce takes will depend on many factors, including how much you and your spouse have to negotiate, how much you can agree on, and whether or not your state has a mandatory waiting period.

The more assets you have, the more complicated the settlement usually is. Even if you agree about how these assets should be split, it still often takes longer to negotiate the agreement than if there were fewer or no assets.

Disagreement about how the assets should be split will cause your case to take more time. Couples who fight over who keeps the house will experience a more drawn-out divorce than if they agree to sell it and split the proceeds.

With children, you will have support and custody issues, whereas if you have no children, there will be that much less to negotiate.

I've seen divorces take less than six months, and I've seen them take years. How long your divorce takes will be contingent on all of the issues just stated, as well as how well you and your spouse can work together, how quickly you gather the facts and figures, and how much you can handle emotionally. The divorce can only move as quickly as the slowest person involved.

How Much Will Divorce Cost?

The cost of your divorce will depend largely on the same factors outlined in the previous section. It also depends on what type of divorce you choose, how much your attorney charges, and what you can afford. One person may be willing to liquidate the college fund or take out a home-equity line of credit on the house to pay for the divorce, and another may not. Couples with no assets to use or liquidate will have to settle sooner than those with more financial resources. The bottom line is that those with more money have more choices than those with fewer assets.

According to an article on *Forbes.com* (Hoffman 2006), the average cost of a divorce is fifteen to thirty thousand dollars per couple. This is absolutely avoidable if you follow the money-saving tips outlined earlier. One woman related to me that she told her attorney, "My budget for this divorce is three thousand dollars, and that's as much as I am going to spend." She got divorced for three thousand dollars. She didn't have children or many shared assets, but the point is that she was assertive, and by sticking to her bottom line, got what she wanted within her budget.

What Should I Expect Emotionally in Divorce Proceedings?

I often hear people say, with the best hopes and intentions, that they believe they will have an amicable divorce and be able to divide assets without any friction. In my experience of seeing hundreds of couples go through this process, it is much harder to sit down and split material and financial assets (not to mention time with the kids) than to think or even talk about it. When your divorce becomes more real, your emotions almost always intensify from the flurry of memories, the pain of the loss, and the fear of what the next chapter of life will bring.

Sometimes, you may even feel angry at your spouse so that you can stay emotionally connected to him or her. This is all a normal part of the grieving process, and no matter how much you have already grieved or how much inner work you've done to prepare for this point, you can't avoid experiencing this new level of emotion if you still care for your spouse or for your lost dream of riding off into the sunset together forever. (Refer to chapter 8 for detailed information on how divorce may impact your children.)

■ *Case Example:* Roseanne and Peter's Story

After nearly two years of separation, Roseanne got up enough gumption to start the legal paperwork to dissolve her marriage to Peter. She was sure that she had already experienced all, or at least most, of her grief and would now be able to move through the formalities relatively quickly and easily.

Filing the divorce papers was a snap. Roseanne even felt some excitement about the idea of having this whole ordeal behind her. She was on cloud nine; that is, until she actually sat down and started gathering all of her accounting for the past five years. When she saw how different their lives had been as a married couple from what life would now be like for her as a single woman, Roseanne was flooded with sadness. She wished her marriage could have worked, even though she had done all she could. Moving on was the best thing for both her and Peter; they were not a good combination. She knew that going through with the divorce was the right next move but, with this new level of emotion to deal with, had some second thoughts.

Peter was also catapulted backward emotionally, which made the negotiations a bit tougher, because his way of coping when feeling sadness was to engage in passive-aggressive behavior. At every turn in the negotiations, he seemed to go out of his way to obstruct the process.

In working with this couple, I let them know that their feelings were normal and that, if they wanted to come through on the other side with the least amount of emotional fallout, they would have to find a way—apart from each other—to acknowledge and express their emotions.

I suggested that they stop looking to each other for relief from pain or for healing. I also reminded them about the difference between unfiltered and filtered feelings (see chapter 3). I encouraged them to allow themselves to feel their authentic grief and stop entertaining the made-up stories that were not serving them.

Although the entire dissolution process was hard on both of them, ultimately they did a very good job of handling their emotions, getting through the division of assets, and finalizing their divorce.

They both had to call on their higher, more mature selves to get through the proceedings, which was particularly challenging since each blamed the other for the downfall of the marriage. Every time they had something major to negotiate, each was tempted to defer to his or her sense of entitlement. Instead, they tried very hard to stay conscious of the big picture and to work together.

What If I Feel the Process Is Not Fair?

You will undoubtedly feel that the divorce process is unjust, regardless of which method you choose (self-representation, mediation, collaborative, or the traditional adversarial approach). Divorce is not fair. It doesn't feel good to have to split time with your spouse to see your children or to divide the assets and sentimental or material possessions. You will feel as if you're getting less, because you *are* getting less: less than what you had together when you were married. Divorce professionals regard "fair" as a nasty four-letter word. The minute you think it should be fair, you will be disappointed, at best.

It's usually wiser to focus on what is reasonable and equitable within the parameters of the law. It's also helpful to give in areas you're not as passionate about as your spouse rather than fight over every little thing. Having a flexible attitude can sometimes inspire a reciprocal desire to give back to you. This can make a world of difference in negotiating the terms of your divorce, as well as in your ongoing relationship with your former spouse once the proceedings are complete.

Setting Postdivorce Goals

How well your divorce goes depends less on how your marriage went and more on your long-term relationship goals. It is not uncommon for couples to actually get along better after the separation, because they no longer have to live in the same house or try to "make the marriage work."

One woman I worked with told me that, despite her extreme anger at her husband for leaving her for another woman, she actually envisioned them getting along, with all of them dining out together some day. She asked me how she could get to that place. I let her know that I thought it would be important for her to refrain from glossing over whatever hurt and anger she still had, but to keep her goal in mind. She would have to do her own inner work and feel her grief, while realizing that, if she wanted a working relationship with him in co-parenting their twins, she would have to stop seeing him as the bad guy.

Through a great deal of counseling, this woman saw her part in why the marriage didn't work, found the ability to move beyond the anger of being left, and eventually formed a nice friendship with her former husband and the new woman in his life.

A turning point for her was when she expressed to me that she wanted to thank him for all that he had done for her in the marriage but was afraid to, because she would open herself to being hurt by him. I asked her what she meant by that, and she revealed that she was afraid that he would throw this back in her face and say, "See all that I did for you?" I asked her what would happen if he did that, and she responded that she would feel vulnerable, as if he had the one up on her.

She touched on something very important in the dynamic of her relationship. During the marriage she had not let him know how much she had appreciated him, which was a big reason why he left. I encouraged her to be generous in acknowledging him and see what happened. She was amazed to see that he not only did not use this against her but also responded very positively. He even thanked her for all she had done for him in the marriage.

Rather than always staying on guard or in protective mode, they both became more vulnerable, which was exactly what was needed to transform their relationship from one filled with bullying and manipulation to one that was kinder and more giving.

On the one-year anniversary of their divorce, the three of them went out to dinner to celebrate their newfound friendship.

I have worked with people who didn't care whether they ended up being friends with their spouses when all was said and done. This certainly isn't a requirement, but it does make life easier for you and everyone around you.

If your focus is not on remaining friends but you have children, it is important to at least be civil. In her book *Mom's House, Dad's House*, Isolina Ricci refers to this type of relating as having a business relationship with your spouse. Dr. Ricci elaborates on this theme by outlining the importance of rules of conduct consisting primarily of simple, basic respect toward each other: conduct such as keeping your feelings in check, honoring the other parent's time (not bringing the kids home early or late, for example), having good enough communication with the other parent (not using your kids to relay messages), and being courteous (Ricci 1980).

If you think of the other parent as a business partner, you can often depersonalize your ex's offensive behaviors, even when you believe he or she is purposely trying to hurt you or make you angry.

Kids' Turn, a nonprofit organization I've worked with that assists children and parents through the difficult transition of divorce, suggests treating your ex as you would a pizza delivery person. He or she hands you the kids, and you say thank you and go inside—impersonal but polite. This type of technique can work wonders when you are dealing with a difficult co-parenting situation.

Exercise: Looking at the Big Picture

On a large piece of art or construction paper, using the longer side as the top of the page, write high on the page, "My Relationship with _____," and fill in your spouse's name. Underneath this title, draw four large circles in a line across the page. In the circle on the far left, write "How It Was." Underneath, list five to ten phrases describing how you and your spouse related during your marriage (for example, "Fought daily," "He was never around," "She was a nag," and so on). In the next circle to the right, write "How It Is." Again, list five to ten phrases describing how you two are relating during the divorce process (for example, "She's being unreasonable," "I'm afraid and don't want to let go," "We can't agree on anything," or "We've made some progress").

In the circle on the far right, write "How I Want It to Be." List five to ten words or phrases that describe your ideal relationship outcome with your spouse (for example, "Amicable," "Good co-parenting relationship," "Forgiveness," or "Civil"). In the remaining empty circle (third from left), write "How We Get There," and then list five to ten actions that you or both of you need to take to reach your goal (for example, "Get co-parenting support," "Time," "More work on myself").

If you can't come up with many words right now, don't worry about it. You can come back to this later, when you have more information or insights about yourself or the relationship.

The importance of doing this exercise is to gain clarity on what kind of outcome you ultimately would like to have. When you know this, you can (and must) begin taking action today to get on that course.

If imagining your postdivorce relationship with your spouse brings up too much emotion, then come back to this exercise later. The truth is, you may never be willing or able to have an amicable relationship with your ex. However, it's important to work toward friendship as a goal, because you will feel better. Being on good terms with the person you were once married to is easier and feels better for everyone involved than the alternative.

Landing on Your Feet

One reason divorce can be so daunting is that, when going into the process, you have no sense of where you will end up and how your life will look on the other side. Most people entering into this vast, unknown territory will imagine negative outcomes.

But how would you feel if you knew at the outset that, once your divorce was completed, both you and your spouse would come through it all okay? I'm sure that most of you would be more confident and less fearful, and you might take action sooner to get to a better place in your lives.

Of all the people I have seen go through divorce, those who get information and support *before starting* the process come out the best on the other side. It may take time, and you may have to do some hard work on yourself, but a good outcome is possible for you too. This book is just one of many resources out there to help you land on your feet.

Exercise: Knowing What and Whom to Ask

Make a list of all the questions you have about separation, divorce, kids, finances, timing, and anything else you can think of. Next to each question, list whom you can contact to answer this question. In some cases, it will be a friend, while in others it will be a therapist, an attorney, or even a book. If you don't know exactly whom to contact for the specific information, ask one of the people on your list if he or she knows whom you can get answers from.

8

Understanding the Needs of Others

Maturity is achieved when a person postpones immediate pleasures for long-term values.

—Joshua Loth Liebman, MD

The last chapter focused largely on your needs once you begin the divorce process, including how to tell your husband or wife that you want a divorce and several of the steps you'll need to take to get through the process.

This chapter discusses more about how to understand the needs of others, primarily your spouse but other family members and friends as well. Knowing what your spouse's needs are and how those needs differ from yours can help both of you more easily navigate the emotional path of divorce.

Also covered are ideas on how to talk and relate to other loved ones—such as your children, other family members, and friends—about your divorce. In the event that you need this, ideas for preserving and redefining all of your relationships are also provided.

Understanding Your Spouse's Needs

Just as the breakup is multilayered, so is the grieving process that accompanies it. At each step, you will feel a new level of emotions. When you first considered divorce, you probably felt some sadness. Then, looking into what divorce entailed likely brought a deeper sadness. Talking to your spouse about it evoked an even deeper level of grief, and seeing his or her reaction likely triggered an even more profound sense of loss.

Now that your desire to dissolve the marriage is out in the open, you may be faced with your spouse's grief on top of your own. It's one thing to merely *feel* that you want out or that the marriage isn't working, but it's quite another when you actually tell your spouse that you are leaving (or vice versa). It obviously makes the split much more real, which is why a new dimension of grief develops. There may be a great deal of fallout, even if your spouse is already aware that the marriage is in trouble and has mutual feelings about divorcing.

As the one who has contemplated divorce for some time, you will probably have experienced most, if not all, of the stages of grief prior to actually telling your spouse that you want a divorce. Unless you have communicated openly with your spouse, sharing your feelings at each step of the process, when your spouse first hears the news that you are serious about leaving, he or she will probably be in a very different place emotionally than you are. Jay and Lisa's story illustrates this point.

■ *Case Example:* Jay and Lisa's Story

Jay was crushed when Lisa told him she wanted a divorce. Because they were in couples therapy, he had assumed they were working on their marriage but now realized that she had no intention of staying wedded to him.

He certainly couldn't argue with the fact that their marriage had been challenging and that they hadn't brought out the best in each other. There wasn't much that they could even compromise on. If he liked something, she didn't, and if she wanted something, he didn't.

Even though, throughout their marriage, they had fought daily about everything from such large issues as where they each wanted to live to such mundane disagreements as at what temperature to set the thermostat, Jay still didn't think that justified terminating the marriage. Having a background with parents who disagreed more than they agreed, Jay had a higher tolerance for fighting.

From Jay's perspective, not only was Lisa ending things prematurely, but she also seemed apathetic about his moving out. To him it appeared that she had simply turned a switch and was done. Jay felt altogether disposable.

Despite Jay's pleas for her to change her mind, Lisa told him that she couldn't change how she felt. She added that she had made up her mind that the marriage was over long before announcing to him that she was filing for divorce. Lisa assumed that Jay had also realized that their relationship was hopeless, and she couldn't understand how he couldn't have seen divorce as inevitable.

Lisa had cried many tears and done the bulk of her grieving long before her announcement came. Jay hadn't done any grieving prior to that point, because he hadn't anticipated the loss. While she was ready to reorganize and move on, he was just experiencing the initial loss.

Your Reaction vs. Your Spouse's

If you have a situation similar to Jay and Lisa's, this is how your respective grieving processes might look:

FIGURE 12: YOUR REACTIONS VS. YOUR SPOUSE'S

YOU	YOUR SPOUSE
Divorce Contemplation	
Initial loss	
Protest	
Despair	
Detachment	

Announcement to Spouse That You Want a Divorce	
Reorganization	Initial loss
	Protest
	Despair
	Detachment

| Deeper loss | Deeper loss |
| Deeper protest, and so on | Deeper protest, and so on |

As you can see from figure 12, when you are the one who has contemplated the breakup for a while, you have a head start on the grieving process. Your spouse may just be starting to feel the loss while you have already been through the detachment phase and are in the reorganization phase.

The person who is being left (the *leavee*) is often in shock from the news (sometimes even when he or she sees it coming) and can't understand how his or her spouse could not be experiencing the same emotions: "How can she be so uncaring?" "How can he move on so quickly?" In the stages of grief, the contrast can sometimes be extreme.

In cases where the initiating spouse (the *leaver*) gets into a new relationship right away, being so easily replaceable can feel like salt in the wound. What your spouse, the leavee, doesn't know is that much of your grieving was done during the marriage. He or she may not have noticed your heartache when you were in the midst of it, and now, even though you may still feel some grief, your grief is at a different, more progressed level.

Because you are the one initiating the divorce, it will be helpful to your spouse if you keep in mind that he or she is not where you are emotionally and needs time to integrate the reality of what is happening.

There are few things in life more hurtful than feeling that the person you married doesn't seem to care about losing you and can replace you in the blink of an eye. Whenever you can, consider your spouse's needs and feelings. It might be easier for you to avoid considering what he or she is going through, but doing so isn't in your best interest.

The following story illustrates how it can actually hurt you to lack empathy for your spouse's need to grieve differently and in different timing.

■ *Case Example:* Maureen and Ian's Story

Without a clue of any major problems in her marriage, Maureen was completely devastated when her husband, Ian, told her he was divorcing her because of his involvement with another woman. Just when she thought it couldn't get any worse, a friend informed Maureen that she had seen Ian out with Maureen's best friend, Ashley.

Suddenly, it made sense why Ashley had been standoffish and why Ian had taken so many business trips lately. Maureen literally felt as if a tractor-trailer had hit her and rolled over her a dozen or so times. She was so devastated that it took her a year just to come out of the initial shock and disbelief.

During that entire twelve months, Ian hounded her to file her paperwork, collect her information, get the house appraised, sign this, and do that. When she tried to tell him that she could barely get out of bed each morning, never mind put together an accounting of her income and expenditures, his response was, "Just get over it. The marriage was over long ago."

Needless to say, she struggled tremendously as her marriage was ripped out from under her. To add insult to injury, she had lost her best friend, who was now living the life she was supposed to be living.

The icing on the cake was that they had to co-parent, and Ian was extremely uncommunicative and uncooperative. There were countless times when Maureen drove to her son's school to pick him up to find that he had already been picked up, and days when the school called her to say that her son was still there because Ian had not picked him up.

Maureen had no idea which end was up, and Ian didn't seem to care. He justified his lack of communication with Maureen by complaining that every time he had tried to talk to her, she had cried or whined about his reasons for leaving, and he didn't want to deal with it.

He was enjoying his new life, and that was all that mattered to him. Maureen couldn't imagine what she must have done for him to treat her so badly, but with such a drastic change in Ian's behavior, the only reasonable explanation that Maureen could think of was that he needed to justify his actions by demonizing her. Perhaps he had even started building his case against her long before he took up with Ashley.

What Ian didn't know or seem to care about was that, had he shown more compassion toward Maureen and how his desire to divorce would impact her, she would have been more present and less stunned, and would have moved through the process more quickly. Rather than getting angrier with her, stopping to apologize would have made a huge difference. Instead, he berated her and saw her as being obstinate.

If you are the one ending your marriage, you are in the driver's seat, and how you handle each step has the potential to steer the entire process. Maureen and Ian's story exemplifies the damage that can happen when each step is not thought through and the other people involved are not fully considered. The importance of having compassion for what your spouse may experience can't be emphasized enough. In the moment it may be easier to tune out your spouse's feelings and try to make them go away, but that will almost always make matters worse.

You don't have to agree, understand, or like your spouse's reaction, but it is in your own best interest to honor his or her process. It's a difficult transition, and the more patience and compassion you can muster for your spouse, the better things will be all the way around.

Understanding Your Children's Needs

This section focuses on how, when, and where to tell your children that you and your spouse are divorcing, and will help you gain clarity on what specific things you can do to take the best possible care of your kids.

The degree to which your children are impacted negatively by your marital dissolution will be contingent not only on what type of marriage you had but also on how the actual dissolution process is handled. In her book *The Good Divorce*, Constance Ahrons discusses the long-lasting harm that can come to children whose parents go through a highly contentious divorce, especially if the children are used as pawns, messengers, or go-betweens (Ahrons 1994). Stories of children being put in the middle are upsetting, like the one I heard recently from a woman whose father had purposely made her tell her mother that he planned to move out. Her mother had asked her what she had done that day with her father, to which she had naively replied, "I helped Daddy find an apartment." You can imagine the response, which, in turn, had made her feel that *she* had done something to upset her mother.

Breaking the News to Your Children

Ideally, you and your spouse will communicate with each other *first*, and both will know about the separation or divorce before your children do. After you have both become clear on what's happening, you will inevitably have to tell your children. Much of how your children will react when you break the news will depend on how you present the information.

In a perfect world, you would talk to your children together as a parental unit, remaining as calm as possible when telling them that you're getting a divorce. In situations where one spouse feels extremely emotional, it's fine to wait until things calm down a bit or have the less emotional spouse do most, if not all, of the talking. You will want to give your children basic information about what's happening and about how the divorce will impact them.

Regardless of your child's age and comprehension level, it is not advisable to lie about the changes that are taking place in the family. Children are incredibly observant. They know more, overhear more, and understand more than you think they do. This has always been true but is more the case today than ever before, mostly thanks to television and movies. Children are growing up faster and being asked to take on more responsibility at a younger age. This is just a side effect of our changing culture. Technology has sped up much of their exposure to life and, in turn, their mental and emotional growth.

Some parents may try to sugarcoat or avoid reality, but in most cases, children see through those tactics. When you tell your children something other than the truth (and this goes for any matter), they learn that their own perceptions are wrong and begin to doubt themselves and their judgments. It's best to be open and honest with your children about the divorce and what it will mean to them.

Having said all this, I don't advise sharing inappropriate details of your marital relationship with your children. The connection you have with your offspring is quite different from the one you have with your spouse and should stay that way. Under no circumstances should you tell your children too much about your marital relationship. And that goes for any child at any age. Parents often treat their children as sounding boards or as they would a good friend, which is simply not appropriate. One twelve-year-old girl I worked with told me that her mother had sat her down and told her that she had not had sex with her father for years. This is way too much for a daughter to know.

Giving your kids information about your divorce on a "need to know" basis is a good place to start, and it is important to allow them to ask questions of both you and your spouse. Anything that they are left to wonder about and imagine won't likely be accurate and almost always demands their taking responsibility where they shouldn't. Let them know clearly that if they have questions at any point, they can ask you.

What to Tell and What Reaction to Expect

Because the questions of what to tell your children and what reaction to expect from them go hand in hand, this subsection is dedicated to simultaneously answering both. For each age group of children discussed, each response is divided into three sections: (1) specifically what to say, (2) what your child's reaction might be, and (3) what children at that particular age need.

While every parent has a distinct style and every child a unique personality, this basic information can act as a guideline to your own discussion with your children.

In a divorce, all the feelings of sadness, fear, anger, or even rage that you or your children might have are normal. They are simply manifestations of the grieving process that everyone involved experiences. Undoubtedly, you will discover that many of the people in your life will grieve, and you each may experience your grief in a variety of ways and at different times. This can be disconcerting to you and may make you question whether or not you are doing the right thing, especially when these emotions never seem to end. But these feelings are not necessarily indications that moving ahead with the divorce is the wrong thing to do. The grief is an unavoidable stage in the divorce process and can compound an already confusing and difficult time.

Even so, of all the humans on the planet, children are the most adaptable and resilient. In most cases (especially if handled sensitively) children ultimately take to the changes very well. This process can take anywhere from a couple of months to usually no more than two years.

Many kids accept that they will have to live in two separate households and often tend to make the best of it, despite the accompanying inconveniences or discomforts. It is we adults who are more set in our ways and can't stand the thought of the children living in two different homes.

How your children react will depend less on their age per se, and more on their developmental process and how you prepare them for the transition. A client of mine with twin five-year-olds found this out when she and her husband split up. For the most part, the girl twin took the news in stride, but the boy twin felt as if his entire world were falling apart. Whatever my client discovered soothed the boy made the girl feel worse, and vice versa. It was quite a challenge for her to meet both twins' needs.

Some kids are born with an ability to see the positive aspects of any situation or "go with the flow," while others are just naturally fearful and anxious. Still others are unusually tuned in and sensitive to the world around them, and always seem to take personally whatever life brings. Keep in mind your own child's needs and temperament as you read on about how children in various age groups react.

How well your child is prepared for the divorce is another important factor. As with an unknowing spouse, if the children have no idea that there are problems on the marriage front, the announcement, "Mommy and Daddy are not getting along and are going to live apart," can come as shocking news. They have had no warning, no time to prepare themselves emotionally, and no indication that what you are saying is true. Kids are extremely resilient, but the best course of action in this scenario is to give them a foundation of information, let them integrate that, and gradually give them more pieces of the puzzle.

Your children may become quite distressed upon hearing the news. The truth is that, like you, many children do get upset in a divorce situation, even in cases where they know it's best for you and your spouse to split.

Unless abuse or neglect is present before, during, or after a breakup, infants often fare relatively well in a divorce situation. This is so primarily because they have less awareness of the intricacies of the relationship dynamics surrounding them, and have no routines that need changing. As long as they have at least one consistent primary attachment figure in their lives and a relatively calm and safe environment, they have a good chance of coming through the transition unscathed. If they have two consistent home bases, they will likely do even better.

All children, regardless of age, are negatively impacted by an angry and abusive environment, so if your marriage had these elements, your children may have been hurt by how they were treated and how they saw you and your spouse treat each other. Any time there is extreme tension at home, regardless of whether it's because of an abusive marriage or a bitter divorce, the children risk coming away deeply wounded emotionally, mentally, and physically.

NEWBORNS TO THREE-YEAR-OLDS

What to say to them: Since infants and toddlers have an extremely limited vocabulary and comprehension level, they may not understand words. However, they will sense heightened emotions, such as increased tension or sadness, changes in schedule or environment, and absence of a parent.

Not only are infants more tuned in to the world around them than older children, they have not yet built up defenses and are thus more sensitive to what's going on in their environments (Hannibal 2000). These very young children will benefit more from physical reassurances—such as being held, touched, and spoken to in soft voice tones—than mental or verbal comforting and explaining.

What their reaction might be: Generally, children between two and three years old may cry when they hear the news but aren't likely to fully comprehend what divorce is until the shifting of homes begins. These children may fear never seeing one parent or the other again. They may have nightmares once the divorce process actually happens, or cry more often and more easily from feeling less contained and safe than when they had both parents living in the same house. They will undoubtedly pick up on your emotions as well and may become more irritable as a result.

The fears usually lessen with time, once these children realize that both parents will come back or that they are being taken care of, but the fears don't always dissipate, especially for highly sensitive toddlers.

What they need: Provide these young children with as much attention and reassurance as you can. If you are extremely emotional and unable to function fully, get help to take care of your young children.

It is extremely hard on children this age to go for long periods (three days is long to a very young child) without seeing each parent, and this should be considered when making the child custody arrangements. If necessary, you can experiment with increasing the amount of time between visits, but the absent parent should be available by phone at least once a day whenever possible. It's best when both parents can provide this sense of safety, but in cases where that is not an option, it will help you to know that infants can thrive with only one primary attachment figure when given consistent care (Hannibal 2000).

FOUR- TO SEVEN-YEAR-OLDS

What to say to them: Children ages four to seven will have a limited understanding of their parents' separation. A standard way to tell your younger children about divorce is something like this: "Mommy and Daddy don't get along, so we aren't going to live in the same house anymore. We will both always love you, and we'll always be your parents. We're just going to live in two different houses, and you will take turns staying with us."

Because children's developmental stages are so distinct in these early years, if you have children in different age categories—for example, a three-year-old and a six-year-old—you may have to have different types of conversations with each of them. This doesn't mean that you necessarily have to tell them separately. In fact, it's probably best for them to be told together at the same time, but the older child will have different fears and reactions than the younger, both of which will need to be addressed.

What their reaction might be: Four- to seven-year-olds will have a greater comprehension of what divorce means. They may cry and ask you lots of questions when you tell them that they will be living in two different houses. It may frighten or excite them, but here again, they will not fully understand what divorce means until it is a reality. These children may believe themselves to be the cause of the separation or divorce, and risk developing a poor self-image as a result of internalizing their pain. They may feel different from their peers because they have a "broken home" (although, with current statistics as they are, divorce is not so uncommon anymore).

What they need: One of the greatest concerns of children between the ages of four and seven will be losing a sense of safety and security (Hannibal 2000). Because they have a limited understanding of what is happening, this age group will need a great deal of explanation of events, as well as reassurance that the divorce is not their fault and that they are loved. They will need to know that you will do everything in your power to have both Mom and Dad nearby and available; however, don't promise anything you can't control or follow through on.

EIGHT- TO ELEVEN-YEAR-OLDS

What to say to them: Older children will comprehend what divorce is about, so you can be more direct and say, "Your dad and I are getting a divorce." You can elaborate more with this age group on what that means or let them know that you don't yet know all the details but that you will do what you can to keep them up to date.

What their reaction might be: Because eight- to eleven-year-olds will have some understanding of divorce, they are more likely to be upset initially. Children at this age now have the developmental capacity to think outside themselves but are still quite self-centered (as they are supposed to be!). They will have a basic understanding that their lives are about to change dramatically and may focus more on how *they* are being put out than on what *you* need or why you divorced. Don't take it personally. Your children are entitled to their feelings. It will help them if you can be a sounding board for them or if they can have access to a professional who has been trained to deal with kids of divorcing parents.

What they need: Generally, the primary concern of older kids is whether or not they will lose contact with one or both parents. They will often benefit from maintaining a strong relationship with each parent.

They are also most likely to believe themselves to be the cause of the divorce and may try to get the two of you back together, because they want everyone to get along (Hannibal 2000). It will be important to reassure them that they didn't cause the breakup, that you both love them very much, and that you will not be getting back together.

If you understand what your children in this age group need and can meet their needs, they will almost always adjust to the transition within several months.

TWELVE- TO SEVENTEEN-YEAR-OLDS

What to say to them: Teens can be told more about what is going on with you and your spouse, but again, it is *never* appropriate to tell your children details of your marital relationship, even when they are older.

What their reaction might be: Twelve- to seventeen-year-olds may also be initially concerned about the potential interruptions or changes to their lives. You may be surprised by how seemingly uncaring they are of your marital status, and because they are older, you may have hoped and expected them to be more understanding. Certainly, a mature teen will have greater compassion for you, your spouse, and any other involved family members, but many adolescents are more focused on themselves.

Teenagers are already individuating (separating themselves emotionally) from their parents and family, so there will be a natural break for them here, which might be exaggerated. Teens are known for testing limits (for example, breaking rules or experimenting with drugs, alcohol, and sex) and may do more of this as a result of having a less-structured family unit.

What they need: The concerns of this age group will include keeping their friends, staying in the same school or after-school programs, and living in the same neighborhood. Keep a close watch on your teenage children. It's important to provide them with firm guidelines and reassurance when needed, to prevent them from feeling alienated, isolated, and alone.

EIGHTEEN-YEAR-OLDS AND OVER

What to say to them: Just as with the younger teenagers, older teens can be told directly that you are divorcing. Even if they don't live at home, they will likely want to know what changes will take place.

What their reaction might be: Divorcing when your children are a bit older might cause them less pain and inconvenience (of course, it also might not), but the biggest advantage is that they will likely have a greater comprehension of the changes the family is undergoing, such as the newly imposed limitations of time, money, and energy that you and your spouse may have postdivorce (Hannibal 2000).

What they need: Older teens need to know what is going on, whether they live at home or not. They need to know how their lives might be impacted.

COLLEGE KIDS

What to say to them: A frank discussion with your children who are in college about the fact that you and your spouse are divorcing is ideal.

What their reaction might be: These children may be impacted by the divorce if they are still connected to you and your home. Obviously, if your kids live at home and attend a local college, they will be affected more directly than if they attended an out-of-state school. College-age children attending school away from home may not be impacted as much emotionally but may feel the financial ramifications if their educations are stopped short, causing them to have to move back home or go out on their own prematurely.

What they need: Ironically, parents who put off divorcing until their children are in college in an attempt to avoid disrupting their lives may have this logic backfire on them. If they are not yet fully self-supporting, these young adults sometimes get upset about not having a stable place to come back to. At a tenuous time in their lives, experiencing additional instability with their original home base can be really stressful and emotionally upsetting. They need to be kept in the loop and treated as if their feelings matter.

ADULT CHILDREN

What to say to them: If you have adult children, you can be more frank about the fact that you are getting a divorce. Telling them too much about your marital relationship is still not a good idea, even though they are adults. Whenever possible, tell your children in person. Obviously, if they live far away, this may not be feasible. It's better to tell them by phone than wait until you see them in person if it is a matter of more than a few weeks.

What their reaction might be: You may be surprised to see your adult children react with a great deal of sadness or loss, but many do. Having a family unit doesn't stop being important, even after your children have moved away from home and perhaps have families of their own.

What they need: Adult children may still need reassurance and the knowledge that they are being considered in any decision making the transition will include.

When Your Kids Ask Why You're Divorcing

When your children ask why you are getting divorced, it's best to let them know in a general way that you no longer get along with each other and that, in such situations, it's sometimes better to live apart. You may want to add that, even though it may be hard for them to understand it all now, you believe you are doing the right thing for everyone in the long run.

This can be challenging to say (and mean) when the cause of the divorce is your spouse's unacceptable behavior. It's also extremely difficult to tell your kids that everything will be okay in the end, when you have similar fears and apprehensions. However, it is critical that you seek out your own support and reassurance, someone you can lean on and vent to in private, who will hold you up and keep you going so that you can prevent your doubts from affecting your children.

I'm not suggesting that you mislead your children, rather that you not share *all* of your fears and doubts with them. Your children should not be asked to bear mental or emotional responsibilities with you or for you.

The Best Time to Tell Your Kids

The question I usually get after "What do I say to my kids?" is "How long before one of us moves out should I tell my kids?" Each situation is different, but in most cases the period between telling your children about your divorce and the actual separation should be from one to three weeks. Less than one week is usually insufficient for such a life-changing event, and more than three weeks is often too much time. Children, especially younger ones, may become anxious if given too much time to wonder when their dad or mom is leaving or what their new house will be like.

An important point to keep in mind when considering timing is that a child's sense of time is quite different from yours. To the majority of us adults, a month is nothing more than a blink, but to young children a month is a big portion of their lives! Likewise, a four-year-old's version of a week differs vastly from a twelve-year-old's, whose version completely differs from an adult's. As we grow older, time passes more quickly. In that month that passed so quickly for you, a preteen might have had two different dating relationships, and a very young child literally has no capacity to think that far ahead.

Even for very young children, anything less than one week is simply not enough time to understand what divorce is, learn about it, and integrate what is about to happen. If children are given too little (or no) notice of the separation, they may feel blindsided, even if there was some indication that this was coming. Although kids are much more resilient than we adults are, with few exceptions it can do more harm than good to burden them with such big news and not allow them time to process it. When children have no time to ask questions or imagine what their new lives may be like, they feel disempowered. This can affect their self-esteem, even much later in life.

Too much notice makes children feel a sense of long-lasting impending doom. Given that a month is a long time to youngsters, they may become more uneasy about the transition as time passes. Your children can't relax because they don't know what's in store. It's so far away that they can't grasp the meaning or what the transition will entail.

Another reason waiting too long can cause problems is that, in situations where you and your spouse have been unhappy for years, prolonging an intended departure can easily turn the unhappiness to bitter toxicity or even abuse, because there is nothing left to lose.

Giving notice of one to three weeks is usually the most optimal time frame for children to adjust to the news, ask questions, and experience their feelings. This is a reasonable amount of time for you and your children to make the transition.

Usually, the more structure you can provide your children at this juncture, the better. It can help your kids feel contained and help you feel that you are in control of the situation. If it is age appropriate and there will be two homes, you can have the children help set up their new rooms or pick wall colors. Offering them choices at a time when they might feel totally out of control can make the situation more tolerable for your children.

Considering Your Children's Schedule

Consider your children's schedule between when you tell your children and when the move occurs. Thinking about what they will have to show up for will be important. For example, if your child has an important recital, a graduation, or a surgery scheduled during those few weeks, he or she will have the stress of this event, the move, the separation, and the uncertainty and won't be able to give his or her full attention to anything.

Waiting until after the holidays, after the beginning or end of school, and after birthdays or special occasions have passed is much kinder to your children. It may be harder for you, because it will require you to contain your emotions and needs. This is not always easy to do when the marriage has truly headed south. If abuse is a real possibility, it may not be advisable to wait. (See the next subsection, "Exception to the Rule.")

If possible, talk to your kids about your divorce when both you and the children have plenty of time for questions and answers, and when you are available to reassure them. For example, the beginning of a weekend is better than Sunday night or a weeknight, when they have homework and have to go to school in the morning.

EXCEPTION TO THE RULE

Although, when one or both parents are ending the marriage, quick exits are not usually advised so that the children can integrate the changes that are taking place, sometimes it is exactly the right thing to do.

I had a client who abruptly moved herself and her six-year-old son out of the abusive, alcoholic home where they lived with her husband. She feared that if she advised her husband of her plan, he would become violent toward her or try to take their son and leave the area (maybe even the country). She couldn't risk it.

One day, while her husband was at work, she departed with her son, leaving only a note behind explaining why they wouldn't be back. She gave no indication of where they had gone or when she would be in touch.

From the moment she and her son moved into their own apartment, she noticed that he began smiling more. Even his teacher at school could not get over the profound difference in his demeanor and learning abilities. He was more alert, more present, and generally happier. Even a recess supervisor who knew nothing about the separation commented to her about what a change she had seen in her son. Leaving was the best decision she had ever made in her life. Exiting quickly was also probably very wise on her part.

In this situation, the court system got involved and helped this woman maintain a safe environment for her and her son. They were able to negotiate the terms of the separation and divorce, and her departure served to help her ex hit bottom and get sober.

In abusive situations it's all too common that leaving without notice endangers those leaving to a lesser degree than if they had stayed. You may have to make some big decisions quickly and on your own, but I urge everyone in this type of circumstance to seek professional guidance through a divorce-support professional. Don't be afraid to ask for help. In most areas, there are local agencies that can assist you. If not, you can conduct an Internet search for information and resources on domestic violence or abuse.

Exercise: Creating a Script

Ideally this exercise is done together with your spouse; however, if that's not possible, it's fine to complete it on your own. This exercise will give you an idea of how to tell your children about your divorce and, if you are nervous about the talk, it will provide the practice you need to hone your skills and choose your words.

A. Start by writing down a script of what you would like to say to each of your children about getting divorced. Write down when you feel it would be best to tell your children and why. Refer to the chart below as a guide for what each child needs for development and temperament according to age.

Age	Need
Infants to three-year-olds	Physical reassurance, such as holding, touch, and soft voice tones
Four- to seven-year-olds	A sense of safety and security
Eight- to eleven-year-olds	Healthy contact with one or both parents
Twelve- to seventeen-year-olds	As much consistency as possible (keeping the same neighborhood, friends, and schools)
Over eighteen years	To be apprised of what's going on and how they will likely be impacted
College-age children	To know that they have a place to come home to
Adult children	Your acknowledgment that it still may be a difficult transition for them

Next, practice your speech out loud so that you can actually hear what it sounds like, but be sure you're out of the kids' earshot. You can say your speech out loud in front of a mirror or record yourself and play back the tape so you can hear it (and also see it, if using video). You may also want to have a trusted friend listen and give you feedback.

B. If motivated to do so, write out the schedule of events your children have coming up and consider when might be the best time to tell them.

Rules of Thumb

Talk openly with your child about his or her needs, fears, thoughts, and so forth; and check in regularly. Then balance that with the needs of both of you, as the parents. Keep in mind that there are many professionals, books, and other resources out there to guide you in setting up a new life for you and your children. (See the suggested reading list at the end of the book.)

Other Factors That Come into Play

Birth order and family role may come into play when older or more-responsible siblings slip into a position of taking care of the other siblings. Younger children may become needier and more dependent on those around them.

Along with each child's personal traits determining his or her reaction to the news of the divorce, studies show that family dynamics also take on a major role. In his book *The Truth About Children and Divorce*, Robert E. Emery shared his research on the impact of divorce on children. He found that children from high-conflict marriages usually fared better after their parents divorced, in part because of the relief that came when the fighting stopped and also because they were not as surprised or thrown off that their parents were splitting up (Emery 2004).

Children whose parents seemed to get along fine have a longer and often more difficult transition period. These children didn't anticipate the divorce, and there was no apparent stress or tension in the home, so having their parents live apart doesn't improve their lives but makes everything harder for them.

■ *Case Example:* Isabel and Bruce's Story

This divorcing couple had three children, ages thirteen, eight, and four, so they had quite a range of developmental capabilities to deal with when they sat their children down to tell them about their separation.

They chose to tell their children on a Saturday morning so they would have the entire weekend to answer questions. Bruce had the kids gather in the living room, and once everyone was seated, Isabel explained, "As you know, your dad and I have been fighting a lot lately. We are sorry about that." Bruce continued, "Because your mom and I can't agree on things, we decided we are going to live apart." He added that he planned to move into a house closer to downtown.

Both parents immediately noticed that the youngest child was getting upset. She thought that her father meant that he would leave forever and she wouldn't see him again. They were able to reassure her that they would always be around her and that her mom and dad needed to be apart so they could get along better.

They gave her an example of when she had fought with a friend at school and how, when children couldn't find a way to share something, they sometimes had to play in separate areas. She still didn't like this, but it made more sense to her.

The oldest of the three wanted to know whether they were all going to move and whether he'd have to change schools. Since Isabel and Bruce honestly didn't know how it would work out in the long run, they told him that, at least in the near future, they did not plan on moving. They reassured him that they would let all of the children know more about changes like this when they themselves knew more. Isabel added that they would not keep any secrets from the kids about what would happen. This statement was particularly reassuring to their son.

The middle girl was mostly concerned about having to share a room. Bruce told her that the place he planned to move into was not as big as the house they were in now and that she indeed would have to share a room with her younger sister. But he added that she could decorate it any way she wanted, which seemed to make her happier.

Twenty-five minutes passed by the time all of the kids' initial questions were answered. Both Isabel and Bruce made it a point to stay around the house for the rest of the weekend, eat meals at home with the kids, and make themselves available to answer any more questions they might have.

They found that mealtime and bedtime were when the kids talked most about their concerns. Although more questions came in the following few weeks, both Bruce and Isabel felt that they had done a good job of addressing each child's concerns at the first meeting while also being candid about what the divorce would mean for all of them in the coming months.

What to Expect After the Dust Settles

Keep in mind that your children's feelings about the divorce may change over time. As I've said, kids are generally quite resilient, but their recovery from the transition is not necessarily a linear process. While in most cases the new lifestyle becomes a habit and life does get easier, there may be points at which the impact of the divorce is greater than at others.

The change in nuclear family, for example, will be especially poignant at your children's important life events as well as at yours and your spouse's. One of the greatest transitions the children may have to make postdivorce is if either of you starts a new relationship or remarries. It can seem as if the shuffling of a deck of cards establishes a new family order.

If you notice any major changes with your children, even a few years after the divorce, pay attention. Because children aren't always able to articulate their feelings (and in some cases don't even *know* what they are feeling), it is important for you to keep an eye on their behavior. The dramatic changes they display may indicate unresolved grief and may require professional intervention.

Examples of behaviors that cause concern include increased crying or moodiness, increased sensitivity, social isolation (even spending more time on the computer, in front of the television, or playing video games), a quiet or depressed demeanor, having a highly negative or self-defeatist attitude, not caring about life, getting poor grades, changing their peer groups, acting out criminally or sexually, becoming verbally abusive, using drugs and alcohol, or becoming increasingly self-destructive in some other way.

If your children seem to be having a tough time adjusting, you can try talking to them about it or asking them what is going on. If they say nothing but you think there really is something bothering them or if they tell you they don't want to talk to you about it, it's usually wise to seek outside help as soon as possible.

Many schools (including most colleges) have free or low-cost on-site counseling. If this type of counseling isn't available, many towns or counties have therapy services that are easily accessible. These will be listed in the phone book as well as online in most cases. Additionally, you can look into private therapy, which can be costly unless covered by insurance, but it can be quite effective in helping your children get through the difficult times.

I suggest that you check in with all of your children periodically as they grow older and let them know that you are always available to talk to them about the impact the divorce has had on their lives.

This overview of how your children will react to the news of the divorce is just that, an *overview*. There are some wonderful books out there on divorce and parenting that go into much greater detail about your children's needs. (Refer to the "Divorce and Parenting" section of the suggested reading list at the end of the book.)

Co-Parenting

Co-parenting is often one of the trickiest aspects in a divorce. Any parenting differences you had when you were married will probably be highlighted once you divorce. Both in my private practice and my work with Kids' Turn (a San Francisco–based nonprofit agency that supports parents and their children through the emotional aspects of divorce), I witnessed the incredible strain caused by having to let go of the child to the ex-spouse.

Concerns included everything from disliking the food one parent served to feeling that the child was not getting enough support with his or her homework to more serious safety concerns. A client once told me that her husband, who had custody of their two-year-old daughter for a day, boasted to her about how well the child had played by herself while he napped on the beach.

As we all know, simply being a parent doesn't automatically qualify someone for the job. Clearly, this father didn't understand the risk he put his daughter in when he dozed off. Some mothers and fathers may need parenting classes to understand the developmental abilities and limitations of their children. Getting the parent who needs the information to receive it is often another story.

Some cases may end up in court, only to have the judge mandate parenting classes. In other situations, a therapist, clergyperson, or sometimes even a good friend can help one or both parents become open to this idea. It can feel like an admission of failure or inadequacy to acknowledge the need for a parenting class, but the reality is that most people get on-the-job training and nothing more. All parents would benefit to some extent from taking structured parenting courses.

A co-panelist at a parent lecture I once participated in passed on this wisdom that had been handed down to him: if parents performed in their parental roles 70 percent correctly 70 percent of the time, they were doing pretty well. The audience laughed in relief.

I tell parents I work with that most of what you learn is in hindsight. Almost all of the challenges your children present will be new for you. You will have to make decisions based on what you guess will bring the best outcome for your children and you.

Parenting is a very difficult and thankless job, but the payoff of having raised some great human beings is tremendous and worth the effort. Co-parenting can be that much more challenging and thankless. But it can also bring two parents closer to each other and to their children.

It's amazing how many parents feel much more eager to see their sons and daughters when they realize that their time together is limited. These parents go farther out of their way to make the visits special. The quality of the time spent together means more than the quantity. In turn, their children often feel more loved.

Understanding Other Family Members' Needs

The task of telling relatives can be distinctly challenging. Sharing the news with parents, stepparents, in-laws, brothers, sisters, stepsiblings, grandparents, aunts, uncles, and cousins leaves you open to persuasion and judgment from those close enough to know something of your relationship but distant enough to be uninformed of the ins and outs of your everyday lives together.

Family members often feel more emotionally invested in the relationship's working out *because* it's family. They may view your divorce as a negative reflection on them and may seem to take the news more personally than nonfamily members do. This holds true for your spouse's side of the family as well as your side.

Maintaining Family Ties

The task of separating from your spouse also entails redefining your connection with his or her family members. This can be challenging regardless of whether they want to maintain a relationship with you *and* your spouse or whether they take sides.

There are several possibilities of how the postdivorce relationships between spouses and family can pan out. If everyone agrees on how that should look, there's no problem. It's when there is disagreement about how to relate to each other that there can be hurt feelings and resentments.

Often, those who have been shut out by their spouses' families and feel a tremendous sense of loss complain that they wish they could explain their sides of the story. They believe wholeheartedly that their in-law relatives would see things very differently (and not close them out) if they could only explain their sides of what happened. It can be quite hard to accept that this opportunity will never come and that you have been extricated from what was your family by marriage.

On the flip side of the coin, I've known some divorcing folks who were upset with their families for *not* taking sides and for remaining friends with their ex-spouses. This usually happens when the ex-spouse has done something unacceptable, such as had an affair, or mistreated or hurt the kids, but I've also seen this expectation of loyalty occur when the relationship comes to a mutually agreed-upon end.

One woman I talked to was very upset that her brother still played golf with her ex-husband. She felt strongly that this was a betrayal to her. But relatives have a right to continue a relationship with your ex if they so choose, and it's not a personal affront (even though it can feel that way!).

This woman made several attempts to stop the relationship from continuing. She warned her ex-husband to stay away from her family, told her family members not to talk to him because of all the awful things he had done to her, and even engaged her mother in trying to put the kibosh on their friendship.

The more she tried to interfere, the more determined her brother and ex-husband were to remain friends, and the less they wanted to maintain a relationship with her. Her tactics not only didn't work, they backfired. This woman was devastated when she already felt lonely and like a failure.

In another situation, a man who'd been excommunicated from his ex-wife's family was devastated to learn that his favorite nephew (on his ex-wife's side of the family) was about to die at a young age. They had been quite close and had not spoken since the divorce two years earlier. He conveyed his dilemma: "Do I honor my ex-wife's wishes that I not see any of her family and possibly make matters worse, or do I risk it and find a way to get into the hospital to see Jake since he's probably going to die soon?"

He went to the hospital just in time to see the nephew, and as it turns out, his ex never found out, but the decision was excruciating for him to make because of the limitations placed on him.

When you have children, there is often more of an expectation and need to stay connected to in-laws, aunts and uncles, and cousins. Interfacing with these relatives after divorce can feel uncomfortable for everyone, and in some circumstances there may be no way around this. However, I believe that speaking openly about defining your new relationship, your feelings of discomfort, and the expectations you now have of each other will help you relax into the new relationship.

It's quite unfortunate, but dealing with other family members can be messy and uncomfortable for years following a divorce. You can't control what happens, but you can let these people who used to be your family know that they are important to you.

Understanding Friends' Needs

The greatest fear people have in telling those not connected by family ties about the divorce is that of being completely rejected. You may well lose some friends when the news of your divorce reaches them. Although it may seem strange to you, this reaction is not as uncommon as you'd like to believe.

Of course, good friends will be supportive of you and understand that your leaving the unhealthy marriage is the best thing you could do for yourself and your spouse, but they may feel some sadness or fear nonetheless.

Regardless of how anyone reacts, you must keep in mind that news of this sort has real or imagined negative ramifications for friends. It almost immediately throws people into a state of self-centered fear. This can be for any number of reasons: they are married and are afraid of catching the "disease of divorce"; they are married and are afraid their spouses might be interested in you as more than just a friend; they are in a very unhappy marriage but don't feel divorce is an option (in this case, they may be jealous and judgmental); they are happily married, and your situation makes them realize that there are no guarantees despite their promises and vows; they are single, and you represented one of the few successful marriages they knew of; or they are single and feel disillusioned about ever finding the right match. There are probably as many reasons as there are people.

If you notice friends distancing themselves from you but you want to maintain the relationships, I suggest talking very directly to each of them about what you've sensed and feel. For example, you might say, "I've noticed that ever since I told you about my divorce, you don't call me as much. I'd like to maintain our closeness. I know it can feel awkward, especially if you plan to stay friends with my ex as well, but your friendship is really important to me."

Some people will feel better about remaining friends with you if they can feel assured that you won't try to put them in the middle. Letting them know that you can keep the relationships separate may be all that they need to hear.

You might also directly ask each friend if there is anything in particular about your separation or divorce that makes him or her feel uncomfortable. This type of open conversation can create a space for your friend to talk about his or her feelings.

If you find that your friend seems defensive or shuts down further in response to this conversation, it's usually best to let him or her know that you won't push the issue but are available to talk further about the situation if or when he or she needs to.

That may be as much as you can do. You can't change how your friends view you or your divorce. Having said that, time often heals some of these issues, and the truly important relationships have a greater probability of enduring your marital dissolution.

Redefining Your Friendships

Once you have sorted out who will remain in your life, you can then work on redefining your relationships. Life as a single person looks and feels quite different than life as a married couple or even a married individual. Just as you see the world differently, others will likely see you in a different light now that you have no "other half." This shift in societal role will require you to find a new way of relating to those around you.

If you and your ex-spouse were friends with another couple and you want to stay friends with one or both people, it is important to have clear expectations of them about how the relationship will look. For some of you, it might help to know that your ex-spouse will be invited to certain functions and you will be included in others, while some of you may not want to know anything about the couple's interactions with your ex.

Staying friends with couples may feel somewhat risky because of the possibility that anything you say or do could get back to your ex-spouse. If you don't care about this, it won't bother you when this happens, but if you do, it can feel unsafe to talk candidly unless you make your needs clear.

Openly stating ground rules, such as "It's okay to share anything I tell you with my ex" or "Please don't tell my ex-husband what we've talked about," can often help. I recommend being clear with everyone, even if you think they already know how you feel. Don't take anything for granted. Stating such boundaries can help redefine your relationship and make the transition much easier for everyone.

Perhaps one of the ways you will be viewed differently as a result of being newly single is *that* you are single! You may now pose a threat to your friends or their spouses. This may not be your intention, but it is a major shift in the dynamics that should not be underestimated.

A woman who attended one of my divorce workshops told me that she was very conscious to avoid calling or visiting her girlfriends when their husbands were around. She wanted to minimize whatever threat she might pose. Where she had once felt free to call her women friends anytime, she now felt the need to prove herself trustworthy and respectful.

Make a list of three or four people whom you consider to be your friends (yours alone or both yours and your spouse's). On the next page, put a check in the box next to the qualities that you feel this friend possesses.

Just as it was important to examine what qualities you valued in your spouse, it can be helpful to understand what qualities you value in friends. This is particularly true after the divorce and as the dynamics shift.

If you value being with interesting people more than their showing loyalty to you over your spouse, for example, then you may not be as upset if they stay friends with your ex. If you value loyalty more than having fun, then you will probably easily let go of seemingly less serious relationships

Name	Loyal	Trustworthy	Dependable	Honest	Deep	Good Neighbor	Fun	Interesting/ Stimulating

9

Making Peace with
Your Decision

*Concerning all acts of initiative and creation, there is one elementary
truth—that the moment one definitely commits oneself, then
Providence moves too.*

—Goethe

Congratulations. You have made a decision. You have been through
quite a lot in coming to terms with whether or not your marriage
could be saved and whether it was even worth saving. But now you know:
you will stay, or you will go.

Despite your fears, reading this book has helped you explore many
facets of your inner self and your relationship. This is hard work, no
matter when you do it, but particularly when contemplating such a major
life change as divorce. The payoff is that you are now clearer about your
truth and life direction.

This chapter explores how you can commit to yourself and your
future, and subsequently what to expect. Regardless of whether you plan
to stay in your marriage or leave, you have made your choice for a reason.
You are exactly where you need to be, and now is the time to trust that

you are making the best choice you can in this moment. You can't see into the future. You can only see the path in front of you, which is all you should focus on.

Committing can feel scary. The "what ifs" pop up all over the place: "What if there's something I didn't consider?" "What if I commit to staying and he slips back into his abusive ways?" "What if I commit to leave and she turns into the woman I'd always hoped she would be?" These are normal reactions when you affirm that you will commit fully one way or another.

Reframing your situation can sometimes make your commitment more comfortable. If you're afraid of committing to feeling this way *forever* but want a reprieve from the back-and-forth of indecision, I recommend committing for a finite period. I suggest no less than six months to a year. This is the time it takes to live with your decision and get more information about your situation. Just knowing that you are headed in one direction instead of bouncing back and forth through life will empower you tremendously.

One reason why divorce contemplation was so crazy making and exhausting was that you second-guessed yourself at every turn. You didn't know what to do, so you did nothing or made halfhearted attempts to stay or go. When you got scared or things got hard, you retreated back to indecision, where you lingered for a very long time. This inaction wore on your self-esteem.

Getting off the gerbil wheel of being neither here nor there will make you feel better and free you up to be more present in every aspect of your life and in every relationship: with your spouse or ex-spouse, kids, friends, work, creative interests, and so much more.

Some of the "what ifs" described earlier in this section may begin to appear. If this happens and your chosen road starts getting rough, you may be tempted to question yourself as you move along. I encourage you to stay firm in your decision to stay married or to separate for the amount of time you committed to, at least for six to twelve months. It's vital to give yourself the time to get some perspective on your situation.

The Difference Between Avoidance and Full Commitment

An important distinction must be made between avoiding an issue (which some try to pass off as having made a decision) and being consciously committed to your decision. You can live apart and remain apart because you don't want to deal with getting divorced, just as you can stay in the same house and go on with the daily routine while pretending you're not in a rut.

Sticking your head in the sand to avoid making a firm decision saps your energy, because you are pushing something away that you don't want to look at. By consciously committing, you embrace your choice and actually become energized. While it may not be easier, it is generally less depleting to you.

One way to know whether you are pushing away or embracing your choice is to check in with your energy levels. If you are tired more often than not, you are probably struggling. If you feel excitement and a sense of renewed energy, you are staying committed to yourself.

Figure 13 on the next page gives some examples of how distinct the behaviors can be when you deal head-on with your marital situation versus avoid dealing with it.

FIGURE 13: DEALING WITH THE DECISION VS.
AVOIDING IT

Options	Stay Together	Separate/Divorce
Fully Committed to Your Decision	Seek couples or individual therapy. Get support from clergy or 12-step programs. Talk more openly with each other. End an affair. Recommit to the marriage. Return to the bedroom. State your needs. Give more. Spend quality time together. Get energy to be more productive.	Seek couples or co-parenting therapy. Seek therapy for your children. Get divorce support. Read self-help books. Become educated about the dissolution process. Move out. Talk to an attorney. Hire an attorney or mediator. File paperwork. Move ahead with a divorce.
Not Fully Committed to Your Decision	Don't talk with your spouse. Don't think about what you want or need. Start or maintain an affair. Get very busy at work. Become more addicted to a substance. Find more reasons to leave the house. Diminish or put down your needs. Justify staying unhappy. Stay for the wrong reasons.	Don't talk with your spouse. Turn the kids against your spouse. Start or maintain an affair. Harbor resentments. Move out abruptly. Often use the "D" word as a threat. Push your spouse away emotionally and mentally. Think only about your needs. Get very busy at work. Become more addicted to a substance. Find more reasons to leave the house.

As you can see from the chart, the activities and thought processes you engage in when you face your situation and commit one way or another will give you energy, because they entail getting information and support. On the contrary, your thoughts and activities when trying to avoid committing sap you of your precious energy, because they include avoiding the situation and not getting enough support.

Exercise: Energy Log

This exercise will help you check in with yourself periodically and see what your energy levels are, as well as track whether or not you are fully committed to your decision.

At the end of each day, write on your calendar a number on a scale of 1 to 10 that represents the overall energy level you felt throughout the day (1 being the least and 10 the most amount of energy). In addition, write a few words about why your energy was high or low.

Person A represents someone who *wants to stay married*, and using the same events, Person B represents someone *who doesn't want to stay married*. You will see the contrast in energy levels these two people experience.

Wants to Stay in Marriage

Person A	7/12	Went to counseling with my spouse. 9 I got honest for the first time about what I needed.
	7/13	I told my spouse I would recommit to the marriage. 7 I'm nervous, but it feels good that we both want to work on "us."
	7/20	Moved into my own apartment to get perspective. 2 This feels terrible and lonely and empty.

Person B	7/12	Went to counseling with my spouse. 1
		It feels like constant pressure, and I always leave feeling worse.
	7/13	I told my spouse I would recommit to the marriage. 3
		I'm saying this more to make him happy than for myself. I feel that a split is inevitable.
	7/20	Moved into my own apartment to get perspective. 8
		This feels exciting. I enjoy not worrying about anyone but myself.

When one month's time has passed, look at your calendar and see what the trend has been. If your energy was at one extreme or the other, why was it that way? Is it clear that you want to stay in your marriage, is it obvious that you want to leave, or are you truly bouncing back and forth between the two choices?

Continue monitoring your energy levels on your calendar to see whether your answer is more apparent over a longer period. I encourage you to share your results with a trusted friend, relative, or relationship professional to get feedback and support as you gain clarity in discerning the right path for you.

Staying in Your Marriage

A great marriage is not when the "perfect couple" comes together.
It is when an imperfect couple learns to enjoy their differences.

—Dave Meurer

You may have just come through one of the toughest periods your marriage will ever experience, but you are now on the other side and are recommitting yourself to your spouse. The escape hatch has been closed, and you have resolved to stay.

No doubt, you feel relieved just in having made up your mind. But, as you well know, this is not the end of the story. In real life, there is no "happily ever after." You will still have to work at your relationship and, in fact, may even have to work harder than you ever did.

If your spouse knew that you contemplated leaving, you may have to work on rebuilding trust. Your spouse may fear that you will change your mind again (and, of course, you can't guarantee that you won't). It is important to reassure your spouse that the option to leave is not on the table right now, and that if you hit another rough spot, your first reaction will not be to look to divorce as an option.

If your spouse doesn't know that you seriously considered leaving, you can probably go on with life as usual. It's up to you whether or not you share with him or her that you had one foot out the door. I believe that, in most circumstances, more openness and honesty almost always serves to deepen your relationship. If your spouse learns how unhappy you've been, he or she may want to do anything possible to respond and make the marriage better.

If you are recovering from a betrayal, it may take more time to rebuild trust. If you betrayed your spouse, you can't rush his or her process of forgiveness and trusting. Even though you know you have committed to staying in your marriage, your spouse can't get inside your head and may remain skeptical or untrusting for quite awhile.

Let me reemphasize the importance of getting some outside support, such as therapy or some type of religious or spiritual guidance at this juncture. Recommitting to your marriage is not a magical cure that undoes problems that have been there for years. Give your marriage time to heal and rebuild. Be patient with your spouse and with yourself.

A marriage (and any relationship, for that matter) is a living entity. If it is not tended to, fed, and watered, it will get sick and/or die. Keeping the life force going between you and your spouse will greatly increase the chances that your marriage will not only survive but also thrive. So, how can you do this?

You learned about the three-step guide to getting your needs met in chapter 5: (1) acknowledge that you have needs, (2) clearly identify your needs, and (3) learn how and where to get your needs met.

These three steps helped you clarify whether or not you could stay in your marriage and, when practiced regularly, can help keep your marriage feeling good and supportive.

■ *Case Example:* Katy and Jean Michel's Story

After months of agonizing over what to do with her marriage, Katy finally decided to stay committed to her husband. She and Jean Michel were in couples therapy, and she was encouraged by some of the changes she saw in him and in their interaction.

Katy made some significant changes in herself as well. Being one of those women who was raised to put the needs of everyone else before her own, she had become worn down to the bone taking care of her husband and the kids, and didn't even realize it until her marriage was in peril.

In my individual work with her, she learned that it was okay to have needs, identified her needs, and understood when to expect her husband to fulfill her needs and when she should go somewhere else to have them met.

She was able to see that Jean Michel wasn't self-centered after all and that she could actually learn to be more like him. He asked for what he needed and wanted, and never apologized for having those needs and wants. She saw that her sarcastic comments to him, such as, "As long as you get what you need, that's all that matters," were unnecessary and only pushed him even further away.

When Katy finally let her husband know that she needed Saturday afternoons "off" to have lunch with friends, shop, take a class, or play golf, Jean Michel was only too happy to spend quality time with the kids. Katy never knew that this was an option because she had never asked. Instead, she had become very resentful of Jean Michel for often taking both weekend days to go off and do his own thing. Because her anger had become venomous, rather than try to understand what Katy needed, his reaction was to leave more often and for longer durations. She actually created more of what she was trying to stop.

After working on their marriage, Jean Michel realized that if Katy even hinted at a snide comment, she needed something that she wasn't getting. He got better at recognizing this trait in her, and in turn she felt safer to be more forthcoming with expressing her needs.

When both of them had something they wanted or needed to do either together or separately, they got better at asking for help outside the marriage, setting up playdates or hiring a babysitter.

Had she not done this work, Katy would never have thought to ask for this time to herself. It saved her marriage. And she knew that if she didn't make honoring her needs a way of life, she and Jean Michel would end up right back where they were before.

With a few exceptions during particularly busy times (the beginning or end of the school year and the holidays), Katy found something to do for herself every Saturday. What, at first, was beyond the realm of her imagination became uncomfortable but doable with more practice. Ultimately, making sure she got her needs met became second nature.

Katy's taking a bit more and Jean Michel's giving a bit more was the key to changing the dynamics in the marriage. It really worked.

Refer to the end of this chapter to complete the exercise "Visioning."

Leaving Your Marriage

There is a time for departure even when there's no certain place to go.

—Robert Frost

Although a divorce may not be the outcome you had hoped for, you probably feel somewhat relieved just in having taken a direction. Life as a divorced person will be hard at first, perhaps harder than you imagined. Yet, staying in your marriage would be hard too.

You will be tempted to question yourself and wonder if maybe you shouldn't leave after all. You may also have peaks of excitement and hope for a bright future. You're stepping out into uncharted territory, and with that you may encounter more emotional highs and lows. This may keep you feeling uncomfortable, but it is perfectly normal.

In time, you will see that life eventually calms down and you find a groove again. How quickly you move through the divorce recovery process will depend on a number of different factors, such as whether it's a mutual decision to split, whether you saw it coming, whether you've been hurt or betrayed by your spouse, whether you have children, how long you've been married, and how emotional you are. In many cases, shorter-term marriages are harder to recover from due to the feeling that there may have been more you could have done, whereas in a longer marriage, you may feel sure that you've done all you could and you may be frustrated that there has been no change despite the interventions. For others, having spent such a large part of your life with your spouse, only to have it end before the "happily ever after" part, can be truly devastating. In these types of scenarios, the loss is not as much about the person as it is the dream and the idea of what it was supposed to look like or the comfort that being part of a family brings.

Your recovery will also be somewhat contingent on how well you get along with your ex-spouse (especially when you have to co-parent), how financially secure you are, and how strong you feel once you're on the other side of the divorce. Struggling to meet your survival and safety needs will almost always prolong your healing process.

How well you take care of yourself and get appropriate support can also be a major factor in how quickly and how well you regain a sense of normalcy in your life. In my experience, finding a group setting that feels emotionally safe can have a synergistic effect, because you are with others who know what you're going through; they can empathize and won't get tired of hearing about your divorce in the way that someone who has never been through it (or has been through it and doesn't want to relive it) might.

How well you recuperate also has to do with your determination to become empowered and learn from the experience. A woman in one of my groups who was initially deflated by the knowledge that she was going to divorce came in one evening and said, "I just don't want this divorce to be the end of my story." Because she made up her mind to feel better about her life when all was said and done, she went from being very down and out to quite strong and empowered. She was still sad and would have traded outcomes in a heartbeat, but was determined to make the best of her life as a newly single woman.

Here again, the three-step process of (1) acknowledging that you have needs, (2) clearly identifying your needs, and (3) learning how and where to get your needs met will help you create the life you truly want to live.

The title of a Joan Lunden book says it all: *A Bend in the Road Is Not the End of the Road* (1998). Divorce is not the final chapter; it's a different chapter. Good or bad, there are many people divorcing these days. You are not alone. You are not a failure. Believe in yourself and in your potential to create the life you were meant to live.

Your Decision and the Hierarchy of Needs

In chapter 5, you learned about Maslow's hierarchy of needs. Married or not, most of us today seek to operate from the higher levels of functioning in the hierarchy. However, when faced with a major problem or life transition, you will naturally feel a threat to your sense of safety, sometimes even with your survival needs brought to the fore. Dealing with marital transition is no exception: your decision to stay or go will affect your current level of need, and it may take some time before you resume your life from the higher levels of love, esteem, and self-actualization.

To expect that you would go right back to functioning from these higher levels once you are over the worst of the difficulties is unrealistic and a setup for disappointment. You can't process the near death of your marriage and simply skip back to "all things normal" just by recommitting to your spouse. You can't begin your life anew as a single person without experiencing many new beginnings.

It will take time to rebuild every aspect of your life. You may not have gone as far down the hierarchy as level one (survival), but you (or both you and your spouse) may have to build up from safety to love, or from love to esteem.

A woman I worked with told me that her husband just expected her to "get over it," because he had decided that he would stay with her after all. Since she had already been through his wanting to leave once before, it was extremely hard for her to believe that all was well and that she could now let her guard down. It took her over a year to feel at ease in the relationship.

When divorcing, you will probably be immersed in survival fears whether or not they are based in reality. Even financially abundant people may have their most basic fears triggered.

A woman in one of my groups admitted to us one day that, despite the fact that she didn't have to worry about money, it was still hard for her to go out and look for a new home, make decisions by herself, and be without someone to "take care of" her. She felt extremely vulnerable and, despite having a more than adequate financial situation, was still up against constant fears of becoming homeless and not getting her needs met.

Splitting assets, finding a new home, and basically having your foundation rocked underneath you can often trigger your core fears. Regression, or going to a lower level of functioning in the hierarchy, is a normal, healthy response to this major life transition.

In time, you will work your way back to trusting that you have all that you need to survive, and will feel safe again. Once healed from the pain you experienced in the marriage and, for those of you not remaining with your spouse, the divorce, you may open your heart again to another relationship. You will feel better about your path and might even be grateful for what you went through. Perhaps it strengthened and deepened you in ways you wouldn't have imagined. You may use your experience to benefit others facing the same challenge, because you may know people who are stuck in the process, be it decision making, divorce recovery, or rebuilding their marriages.

In fact, you may fear getting stuck too. But you can avoid this by allowing yourself to experience your unfiltered feelings, your true grieving process, and stopping yourself from entertaining untrue stories. You can choose the lens through which you see your circumstances.

When faced with the major challenges life throws your way, you can learn their inherent lessons, or you can miss them. If you miss them, they will probably come back around again. The most common lessons that I see people needing to learn from relationships are how to communicate what is going on inside of them and how to ask for help.

Sean was a CEO for a large corporation. His job entailed enormous responsibilities, not just locally but all over the world. He saw himself as the go-to guy for any problems or concerns within the corporation. He was always available and never seemed to need anything himself.

However, when his wife of twenty-seven years left him, his armor cracked. No longer could Sean play the strong one, because he hurt too deeply. But having long played the role of being in charge, helping others, and having "broad shoulders," he felt he couldn't let anyone know that he had needs, so he attempted to maintain a strong facade. Finally, he had a nervous breakdown and was admitted into a local psychiatric hospital.

Because he had to, Sean finally developed the ability to show others his vulnerabilities and ask for the support he needed. At last, he could be more authentic and stop trying to be superhuman. Had this breakdown not happened, Sean would have continued to pressure himself to pull himself up by the bootstraps and not let his "weaknesses" (as he called them) leak out.

Ironically, one of the reasons his wife left him was that she felt she didn't know him. When she found out that he was in the hospital, she went to see him, and they had a conversation unlike any other they had ever had before. He was more real and present than she'd ever seen him. He was now willing to get into the marital counseling that she had tried to get him to attend so many times before, and they were ultimately able to salvage their marriage.

Sean told me that he thought he had needed these events to get his attention so that he could change. He got the lesson that he needed to be more open. After some time off to focus on himself and his marriage, he got his life back and had a much healthier perspective on everything.

Exercise: Looking Back to See Forward

Writing in your journal and reflecting can help bring closure to your decision-making process. This exercise asks you to think about what you've learned about yourself through reading this book. What did you gain from your marriage, and how would you like to apply that knowledge to the next chapter of your life?

These questions tie in with the three-step guide mentioned earlier. This three-step process is one you can come back to any time you feel yourself slipping back into an unhealthy dynamic with those around you. It will help you sort out what you need, how to get your needs met, and who should meet them.

Feel free to add your own questions or statements to this exercise.

1. I learned to acknowledge _____.

2. I learned that I needed _____.

3. I learned to pay attention to _____.

4. I got clearer with _____.

5. I learned to get my needs met by (write the method and people you go to now) _____.

6. Learning and practicing this has helped me because _____
    _____.

If you had trouble answering these questions, you may want to review chapter 5 and come back to this. The three-step process takes some getting used to and practice before it takes hold.

Exercise: Visioning

At the end of each of my Contemplating Divorce workshops, I have the attendees get comfortable in their chairs; close their eyes; look five, ten, or twenty years into the future; and answer the following questions:

1. Where do you want to be?

2. How do you want your life to be?

3. What do you want to be able to say that you accomplished?

4. Upon your deathbed, what would you regret not having done?

5. What can you do today to get closer to your true life's purpose?

You can repeat this exercise every month or every day if you'd like. It's important to spend some time pondering what you want to create in your life, and then take the necessary steps to get closer to your dreams.

Your Remaining Journey

With either choice you make—to stay in your marriage or dissolve it—you may always have moments of doubting that you made the right decision. Don't panic and don't necessarily give in to this idea. You are agreeing to give yourself six months to one year (or whatever time frame you've allotted) to just stick with your decision, so unless your situation becomes intolerable, it's important to give yourself that time. In all likelihood, you will have a very different perspective when the period has ended.

It is my hope that this book will help lift you out of the quagmire of indecision to a place of power from which to fully live, love, and commit to yourself, regardless of which road you choose. Allowing yourself to be swayed by indecision keeps you weak. When you have direction, you have strength. I wish you all the best on your journey.

Suggested Reading

Understanding Relationships

Brizendine, Louann. 2007. *The Female Brain.* New York: Broadway Books.

de Angelis, Barbara. 1998. *Are You the One for Me?* New York: Harper Thorsons Element.

Evans, Patricia. 1996. *The Verbally Abusive Relationship: How to Recognize It and How to Respond.* Avon, MA: Adams Media Corporation.

Goleman, Daniel. 2007. *Social Intelligence: The Revolutionary New Science of Human Relationships.* New York: Bantam Dell Publishing Group.

Gray, John. 2004. *Men Are from Mars, Women Are from Venus: The Classic Guide to Understanding the Opposite Sex.* New York: HarperCollins Publishers, Inc.

Stone, Hal, and Sidra Stone. 1989. *Embracing Each Other: How to Make All Your Relationships Work for You.* Albion, CA: Delos Publications.

———. 2000. *Partnering: A New Kind of Relationship—How to Love Each Other Without Losing Yourselves.* Novato, CA: Nataraj Publishing.

Welwood, John. 2006. *Perfect Love, Imperfect Relationships: Healing the Wound of the Heart.* Boston: Trumpeter Books.

Williamson, Marianne. 2001. *Enchanted Love: The Mystical Power of Intimate Relationships.* New York: Touchstone.

Contemplating Divorce

Kirshenbaum, Mira. 1997. *Too Good to Leave, Too Bad to Stay: A Step-by-Step Guide to Help You Decide Whether to Stay In or Get Out of Your Relationship.* New York: Plume.

Raffel, Lee. 1999. *Should I Stay or Go? How Controlled Separation (CS) Can Save Your Marriage.* Chicago: Contemporary Books.

Williamson, Marianne. 2006. *Power to Change.* Carlsbad, CA: Hay House, Inc. CD-ROM.

Saving Your Marriage

Gottman, John M. 1995. *Why Marriages Succeed or Fail: And How You Can Make Yours Last.* New York: Fireside.

———. 2001. *The Relationship Cure: A Five-Step Guide to Strengthening Your Marriage, Family, and Friendships.* New York: Three Rivers Press.

Gottman, John M., and Nan Silver. 2004. *The Seven Principles for Making Marriage Work.* London: Orion Publishing Group.

Jacobs, John W. 2005. *All You Need Is Love and Other Lies about Marriage: How to Save Your Marriage Before It's Too Late.* Toronto: Perennial Currents.

Raffel, Lee. 2002. *Saving Your Marriage: Separate to Rejuvenate Your Relationship.* New York: MJF Books.

Solomon, Steven D., and Lorie J. Teagno. 2006. *Intimacy After Infidelity: How to Rebuild and Affair-Proof Your Marriage.* New Harbinger: Oakland, CA.

Spring, Janis A. 1997. *After the Affair: Healing the Pain and Rebuilding Trust When a Partner Has Been Unfaithful.* New York: Harper Perennial.

Weiner-Davis, Michele. 1993. *Divorce Busting: A Step-by-Step Approach to Making Your Marriage Loving Again.* New York: Fireside.

———. 2002. *The Divorce Remedy: The Proven Seven-Step Program for Saving Your Marriage.* New York: Fireside.

During and After Divorce

Fisher, Bruce, and Robert Alberti. 2005. *Rebuilding: When Your Relationship Ends.* 3rd ed. Atascadero, CA: Impact Publishers.

Ford, Debbie. 2001. *Spiritual Divorce: Divorce as a Catalyst for an Extraordinary Life.* San Francisco: HarperSanFrancisco.

Lunden, Joan, and Andrea Cagan. 1998. *A Bend in the Road Is Not the End of the Road: Ten Positive Principles for Dealing with Change.* New York: William Morrow.

Mercer, Diana, and Marsha Kline Pruett. 2001. *Your Divorce Advisor: A Lawyer and a Psychologist Guide You Through the Legal and Emotional Landscape of Divorce.* New York: Fireside.

Smoke, Jim. 1995. *Growing Through Divorce.* Eugene, OR: Harvest House Publishers.

Divorce and Parenting

Ahrons, Constance. 1994. *The Good Divorce: Keeping Your Family Together When Your Marriage Comes Apart.* Hardcover ed. New York: HarperCollins.

Emery, Robert E. 2004. *The Truth About Children and Divorce: Dealing with the Emotions So You and Your Children Can Thrive.* New York: Penguin Group.

Hannibal, Mary Ellen. 2007. *Good Parenting Through Your Divorce: The Essential Guidebook to Helping Your Children Adjust and Thrive—Based on the Leading National Program.* 2nd ed. New York: Marlowe & Company.

Jones-Soderman, Jill, and Allison Quattrocchi. 2006. *How to Talk to Your Children About Divorce: Understanding What Your Children May Think, Feel, and Need.* Scottsdale, AZ: Family Mediation Center Publishing.

Ricci, Isolina. 1980. *Mom's House, Dad's House: Making Two Homes for Your Child—A Complete Guide for Parents Who Are Separated, Divorced, or Remarried.* 1st ed. New York: Fireside.

———. 2006. *Mom's House, Dad's House for Kids: Feeling at Home in One Home or Two.* New York: Fireside.

Ross, Julie, and Judy Corcoran. 1996. *Joint Custody with a Jerk: Raising a Child with an Uncooperative Ex.* New York: St. Martin's Press.

Divorce and Finances

Coullahan, Joan, and Sue van der Linden. 2002. *Financial Custody: You, Your Money, and Divorce.* Indianapolis, IN: Alpha Books.

Rosenwald Smith, Gayle. 2004. *Divorce and Money: Everything You Need to Know.* New York: Perigree.

Nolo Books

Nolo is a publishing company based in Berkeley, California, that was founded in 1971 with the mission of making the legal system more user friendly, affordable, and accessible to all Americans.

Doskow, Emily. 2006. *Nolo's Essential Guide to Divorce.* Berkeley, CA: Nolo.

Sherman, Ed. 2003. *Divorce Solutions: How to Make Any Divorce Better.* Berkeley, CA: Nolo Press Occidental.

————. 2007. *How to Do Your Own Divorce in California: Everything You Need for an Uncontested Divorce.* 30th ed. Berkeley, CA: Nolo.

Stoner, Katherine E. 2001. *Using Divorce Mediation: Save Your Money and Your Sanity.* Berkeley, CA: Nolo.

Woodhouse, Violet, and Dale Fetherling. 2006. *Divorce and Money: How to Make the Best Financial Decisions During Divorce.* Berkeley, CA: Nolo.

References

Ahrons, Constance. 1994. *The Good Divorce: Keeping Your Family Together When Your Marriage Comes Apart.* Hardcover ed. New York: HarperCollins.

Coontz, Stephanie. 2005. *Marriage, a History: How Love Conquered Marriage.* New York: Penguin Group.

Emery, Robert E. 2004. *The Truth About Children and Divorce: Dealing with the Emotions So You and Your Children Can Thrive.* New York: Viking Penguin.

Ford, Debbie. 2005. Thank god for your discontent. *Best Year of Your Life* electronic newsletter, June 1. By subscription only.

Hannibal, Mary Ellen. 2002. *Good Parenting Through Your Divorce: How to Recognize, Encourage, and Respond to Your Child's Feelings and Help Them Get Through Your Divorce.* 1st ed. New York: Marlowe & Company.

Hicks, Esther, and Jerry Hicks. 2004. *Ask and It Is Given: Learning to Manifest Your Desires.* Carlsbad, CA: Hay House.

Hoffman, Leah. 2006. Smart ways to save money in a divorce: Best advice—try to end things amicably, avoid high legal fees. *Forbes.com,* Nov. 17, 2006, http://www.msnbc.msn.com/id/15753189.

Kübler-Ross, Elisabeth. 1969. *On Death and Dying.* New York: Touchstone.

Lee, Felicia R. 1996. Influential study on divorce's impact is said to be flawed. *New York Times,* May 9, 1996, Home and Garden section, online ed., http://query.nytimes.com/gst/fullpage.html?res=9C07E6DCI539F 93AA35756C0A960958260.

Lunden, Joan, and Andrea Cagan. 1998. *A Bend in the Road Is Not the End of the Road: Ten Positive Principles for Dealing with Change.* New York: William Morrow.

Maslow, Abraham. 1943a. A theory of human motivation. *Psychological Review* 50(4), as quoted by Christopher D. Green, http://psychclassics .yorku.ca/Maslow/motivation.htm. Accessed January 2008.

————. 1943b. *Motivation and Personality.* New York: Harper & Row.

Raffel, Lee. 1999. *Should I Stay or Go? How Controlled Separation (CS) Can Save Your Marriage.* Chicago: Contemporary Books.

Ricci, Isolina. 1980. *Mom's House, Dad's House: Making Two Homes for Your Child—A Complete Guide for Parents Who Are Separated, Divorced, or Remarried.* 1st ed. New York: Fireside.

Satterfield, Jason. 2007. Self-destructive emotions. Workshop at Institute for Brain Potential, LBP, Los Altos, CA.

Walker, Lenore. 1979. "The Cycle of Domestic Violence" Diagram in *The Battered Woman.* New York: Harper & Row.

Susan Pease Gadoua, LCSW, is the founder and executive director of the Transition Institute of Marin, an agency that provides coaching, therapy, and workshops to people who are at some stage of marital dissolution. She has been working with divorced or divorcing couples and individuals for nearly a decade. Pease Gadoua lives in the greater San Francisco Bay Area with her husband and two dogs.

more books from new**harbinger**publications, inc.

COUPLE SKILLS, SECOND EDITION

Making Your Relationship Work

US $17.95 / ISBN: 978-1572244818

WHEN GOOD MEN BEHAVE BADLY

Change Your Behavior, Change Your Relationship

US $16.95 / ISBN: 978-1572243460

COPING WITH YOUR PARTNER'S JEALOUSY

US $12.95 / ISBN: 978-1572243682

THE HIGH-CONFLICT COUPLE

A Dialectical Behavior Therapy Guide to Finding Peace, Intimacy & Validation

US $15.95 / ISBN: 978-1572244504

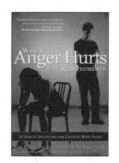

WHEN ANGER HURTS YOUR RELATIONSHIP

Ten Simple Solutions for Couples Who Fight

US $16.95 / ISBN: 978-1572242609

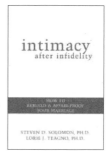

INTIMACY AFTER INFIDELITY

How to Rebuild & Affair-Proof Your Marriage

US $14.95 / ISBN: 978-1572244610

available from

new**harbinger**publications, inc.

and fine booksellers everywhere

To order, call toll free **1-800-748-6273** or
visit our online bookstore at **www.newharbinger.com**

(VISA, MC, AMEX / prices subject to change without notice)